T0298828

TOWARDS A PEOPLE-DRIVEN
AFRICAN UNION
CURRENT OBSTACLES & NEW OPPORTUNITIES

January 2007

(Updated November 2007)

First published 2007 by the African Network on Debt and Development (AFRODAD), the Open Society Institute Africa Governance Monitoring and Advocacy Project (AfriMAP), and Oxfam GB.

Second edition published November 2007 by the African Network on Debt and Development (AFRODAD), the Open Society Institute Africa Governance Monitoring and Advocacy Project (AfriMAP), and Oxfam GB.

Copyright © 2007 African Network on Debt and Development, Open Society Initiative for Southern Africa and Oxfam GB.

All rights reserved. Redistribution of the material presented in this work is encouraged by the publisher, provided that the original text is not altered, that the original source is properly and fully acknowledged and that the objective of the redistribution is not commercial gain. Please contact info@afrimap.org if you wish to reproduce, redistribute or transmit, in any form or by any means, this work or any portion thereof.

British Library Cataloguing in Publication Data: A catalogue record for this book is available from the British Library

ISBN (soft-cover) 978-1-920051-83-9
ISBN (Ebrary): 978-1-920489-60-1
ISBN (MyiLibrary): 978-1-920489-61-8
ISBN (Adobe PDF digital edition): 978-1-920489-62-5

Production and print management by COMPRESS.dsl www.compressdsl.com

Distributed by African Minds,4 Eccleston Place, Somerset West, 7130, South Africa
info@africanminds.co.za
www.africanminds.co.za

ORDERS:
African Books Collective
PO Box 721, Oxford OX1 9EN, UK
orders@africanbookscollective.com
www.africanbookscollective.com

CONTENTS

ACKNOWLEDGEMENTS

This report was researched and written by Ibrahima Kane and Nobuntu Mbelle. It was edited by Bronwen Manby (AfriMAP) and Peter da Costa. Bronwen Manby, Irungu Houghton (Oxfam GB), Pascal Kambale (AfriMAP), Vitalis Meja (AFRODAD), and Ozias Tungwarara (AfriMAP) were members of the steering committee that guided the research and drafting process. The authors and steering committee would like to thank the staff from the African Union Commission, embassies and ministries of foreign affairs, and civil society organisations who were interviewed in the course of this research, attended the workshop in Addis Ababa to discuss its findings, or commented on the draft text. All contributions are greatly appreciated; those who made a contribution are listed in the annex to the report. While the detailed findings and recommendations do not necessarily reflect the official position of all the commissioning and endorsing organisations, we collectively believe that they make a positive contribution to an open and publicly accountable African Union.

Endorsing organisations

ACORD (Agency for Cooperation and Research in Development)
ActionAid International
AMWIK (Association of Media Women in Kenya)
Chambers of Justice
CREDO (Centre for Research Education and Development of Rights in Africa)
Darfur Consortium
Equality Now
FAHAMU
FPIF (Foreign Policy in Focus)
ICHIRA (International Centre for Health Interventions and Research in Africa)
IRTECO (Irrigation Training and Economic Empowerment Organisation, Tanzania)
KAACR (Kenya Alliance for the Advancement of Childrens Rights)
KETAM (Kenya Treatment Access Movement)
MWENGO (Mweleko wa NGO)
Pan African Movement
RADDHO (Recontre Africaine pour la Défense des Droits de l'Homme)
UMANDE Trust, Kenya
UN Millennium Campaign
World Vision International

LIST OF ACRONYMS

AfriMAP	African Governance Monitoring and Advocacy Project
AFRODAD	African Forum and Network on Debt and Development
APRM	African Peer Review Mechanism
AU	African Union
CIDO	African Citizens' Directorate (of the AU Commission)
CREDO	Centre for Research Education and Development of Rights in Africa
CSO	civil society organisation
CSSDCA	Conference for Security, Stability, Development and Cooperation in Africa
ECOSOCC	Economic, Social and Cultural Council
ECOWAS	Economic Community of West African States
FEMNET	African Women's Development and Communication Network
NEPAD	New Partnership for Africa's Development
NGO	non-governmental organisation
OAU	Organisation of African Unity
PRC	Permanent Representatives Committee
RADDHO	*Rencontre Africaine pour la Défense des Droits de l'Homme*
REC	Regional Economic Community
SADC	Southern Africa Development Community
SADC-CNGO	SADC Council of Non-Governmental Organisations
SOAWR	Solidarity for African Women's Rights
UN	United Nations
WACSOF	West African Civil Society Forum

Preface: Background to this study

This research report was jointly commissioned and coordinated by Oxfam GB, the African Network on Debt and Development (AFRODAD), and the Africa Governance Monitoring and Advocacy Project (AfriMAP), an initiative of the Open Society Institute network of foundations in Africa.[a]

In January 2006, the three organisations agreed to examine and compare the extent of national policy and public engagement around the bi-annual summits[b] of the African Union (AU) at the AU headquarters in Ethiopia and in a sample of African countries. The African Union has already developed a reputation for charting an ambitious pan-African state-building project, yet very little is understood by policy-makers or citizens of how African countries prepare for the summits and their related ministerial meetings, and how they implement decisions and resolutions made in these fora. As a consequence, African citizens are not able to contribute effectively to the building of the pan-African institutions, which remains a project largely restricted to a small elite.

Since the AU Commission is now near the end of the first phase of its strategic plan (2004–2007), it seemed a good moment to ask questions designed to draw lessons for the next stage of continental institution-building. What are some of the best practices that have contributed to effective intra-state coordination, consultation with non-state national actors and public accountability? Are there major divergences between African countries in the way they organise around African summits and international summits? What policy and practice changes could be proposed to improve the quality of continental policy-making and implementation? What could civil society organisations and citizens do to contribute effectively to this process? How can the AU be made more open and transparent to African citizens?

During 2006, two researchers interviewed respondents from among civil society and government officials from 11 countries,[c] and attended both the January and July summits in Khartoum and Banjul, to find answers to these questions and draft a report of their findings. A consultative meeting to discuss the draft report prepared from this research was held in Addis Ababa, Ethiopia on 10–11 November 2006 and attended by representatives of member states, the AU Commission and civil society organisations. Inputs from this meeting were incorporated into the draft final text, which was then circulated to a wide range of African civil society organisations and coalitions for their comment and endorsement.

The scope of the study has been limited to preparations for AU summits, broadly speaking, in order to keep a tight focus on one set of issues. We have thus not included discussion of civil society engagement with several other important African Union structures, including the Peace and Security Council, the secretariat for the New Partnership for Africa's Development (NEPAD), the African Peer Review Mechanism, the Pan-African Parliament, or the African Commission on Human and Peoples' Rights. Much would no doubt be learned by extending research to these organs, as well as to other countries, especially the island states and others rarely studied for such purposes, and other regional economic communities.

The three commissioning organisations are committed to the vision of the African Union as an institution open and accountable to all Africa's citizens. We offer this research as a contribution to achieving that aim.

Postscript, November 2007: The report was launched at the January 2007 summit of the African Union. This is an updated edition, with an additional chapter 10 providing information on events during 2007. The text is otherwise unchanged.

VISION AND MISSION OF THE AFRICAN UNION, MAY 2004

The vision of the African Union is that of an Africa integrated, prosperous and peaceful, an Africa driven by its own citizens, a dynamic force in the global arena.

1. FINDINGS AND RECOMMENDATIONS

This report presents research on the preparations for and conduct of African Union summits, from some of the civil society organisations currently working with the African Union to realise its own vision. It concludes that, although significant space has been opened up for greater and more sustained participation by a diversity of interested groups, the promise of a people-driven African Union (AU) remains largely unfulfilled. Inadequate institutional capacity and inappropriate policies and procedures have hindered the realisation of the vision that the AU should build 'a partnership between governments and all segments of civil society ... to strengthen solidarity and cohesion among our peoples'.

The advent of the AU in 2001 raised hopes of a strong, united continent composed of peaceful, democratic states respectful of good governance, human rights and the rule of law. The establishment of new organs, including the Peace and Security Council, the Pan-African Parliament and the Economic, Social and Cultural Council (ECOSOCC), as well as the AU's absorption of the New Partnership for Africa's Development (NEPAD) and the African Peer Review Mechanism (APRM), added to the widespread belief that a new African era could be in the making.

For virtually the first time since the founding of the AU's predecessor, the Organisation of African Unity (OAU), in 1963, African civil society was recognised as an important player in developing the continent. Nowhere was this more evident than in the inclusion of ECOSOCC in the organs created by the AU Constitutive Act, giving civil society representatives a formal advisory role in AU institutions and decision-making processes.

On a number of fronts, the mood was optimistic. The setting up of the Pan-African Parliament in March 2004 provided further affirmation that, unlike the OAU, the AU would operate on the basis of a decentralised model with several sources of authority. On his appointment to head the AU Commission in 2002, Chairperson Alpha Konaré reiterated his personal commitment to involving civil society in the development of the Commission's vision and mission. Key civil society organisations reoriented their programmes around AU priorities.

However, many institutional obstacles still block the realisation of the African Union's original vision. There is a growing perception among civil society organisations that the initial AU enthusiasm for non-state participation in its policy development processes has given way to a more closed stance. Despite the reorganisation of the former OAU secretariat into the AU Commission, many staff seemed to retain their old habits and attitudes. There are still considerable difficulties in obtaining access to information about policies and documents under discussion by AU organs, preventing effective participation by Africa's citizens in continental decision-making processes.

Moreover, as this report shows, the sheer proliferation of AU ministerial meetings, ordinary and extraordinary summits is taking a heavy toll on both the AU Commission and governments. Unless Commission budget shortfalls and capacity constraints in member states are remedied, the African Union will not be able to deliver on the promise of its decisions, resolutions and treaties. The report calls on the African Union Commission and member states to take urgent action to simplify and improve the multiplicity of legal frameworks, incoherent institutional arrangements and unclear policies and procedures, and to provide more consistent and timely access to documentation in all its processes.

The planned review of the working methods of the AU's institutions constitutes an important opportunity to regain momentum. To this end, the findings and recommendations below are offered in the hope that they can contribute constructively to this process.

Member states

The office of the president and ministry of foreign affairs are the key agencies in most countries for preparations for AU summits. The ambassadors based in Addis Ababa, who sit on the Permanent Representatives Committee (PRC) of the AU, form the critical link between national governments and the AU institutions.

Many of the national policy-makers interviewed for this report clearly acknowledged the significance of the transition from the OAU to the AU. Yet we found little evidence at the national level of steps taken to put in place institutions and processes that respond to the new continental architecture. Only a few states prepare adequately for the AU summits. In some cases, lead ministries relevant to thematic issues being discussed at a summit had not been informed or their input sought. The capacity of governments and Addis Ababa embassies to collate, analyse and distribute information was identified as a serious constraint.

Of significant concern is the almost total absence of efforts by national executives to engage parliament or civil society organisations in discussions around national positions.

Member states should thus broaden and deepen their consultation processes in advance of summits, both to ensure that all relevant ministries and agencies are informed of issues to be debated, and to brief parliament, the media and civil society about issues on the AU agenda and proposed national positions.

Recommendations for member states at national level

1. Ministries of foreign affairs should ensure that all relevant ministries and other branches of the executive are informed about and invited to contribute on the agenda items that concern them at forthcoming summits. This may require providing additional staff at embassies in Addis Ababa whose responsibility it is to collate and forward material related to AU business to the appropriate agencies.

2. Ministries of foreign affairs should also broaden the set of institutions that contribute to the development of national positions on AU policy proposals. This should include relevant parliamentary committees, constitutional bodies such as national human rights institutions, ECOSOCC national chapters, the media and other fora organised by civil society organisations. 'Best practices' in this regard should be encouraged in all member states.

3. In civil law countries where the responsibilities of government departments are regulated by decree, states should update these decrees to reflect the new institutions of the African Union.

4. Member states should create civil society/ECOSOCC focal points in their departments of foreign

affairs and provide guidance to embassies in Addis Ababa to respond to requests for information from civil society organisations.

5.   Member states should meet assessed financial contributions to the AU. Failure to do so undermines the AU Commission's ability to fulfil its responsibilities.

Conduct of and follow-up to summits

Decisions taken in meetings of the Permanent Representatives Committee, Executive Council of Ministers and Assembly of Heads of State and Government are key to the success or failure of the African Union and its institutions. Yet the report finds that there is no effective mechanism to monitor and ensure implementation of decisions taken at summits. This vacuum threatens to undermine the entire purpose of the AU.

The recently introduced practice of holding two summits a year places great stress on the administrative capacity of the AU Commission to prepare for and implement the decisions of the heads of state. Many decisions require other meetings to be organised to develop policies and implementation strategies, so that the entire time of the Commission can be taken up in organising meetings. Furthermore, member states often fail to respect rules of procedure in relation to summit preparations and conduct, increasing the administrative burden. The distribution of preparatory documentation prior to summits was described by one diplomat as 'catastrophic'. Many spoke about agenda items not being adequately considered by member states before the summit is required to make a decision upon them.

The role of the regional economic communities (RECs) at summits is unclear. In addition, because membership of the RECs is not the same as the regional political blocs within the Permanent Representatives Committee, it is difficult to understand how African regions form common positions and can be held publicly accountable at the AU-level.

Inadequate obligations on states hosting the summits to be open to civil society participation and unclear rules of accreditation continue to limit African citizens' access to AU summits. Civil society leaders interviewed for the report recounted their recurrent difficulties in obtaining visas to enter the country where the summit is being held, accreditation to attend meetings, or even meeting space to hold civil society discussions alongside the summits.

Procedures around preparations for summits need to be revised and strengthened so that fewer meetings are held and so that deadlines for submission and distribution of documents are adhered to. Either more resources need to be allocated to the Commission by member-states or the number of summits should be reduced to one each year. Follow-up mechanisms to summits must also be strengthened as a means to ensure better compliance with and effectiveness of summit resolutions.

Recommendations for member states in AU decision-making fora

Member states, in the appropriate meetings of the Permanent Representatives Committee, Executive Council of Ministers and Assembly of Heads of State and Government, should:

6.   Establish a committee of the PRC to monitor implementation of decisions by AU organs and report to the Assembly at each summit, in order to ensure better compliance and effectiveness of AU decision-making, and instruct the AU Commission to prepare reports for this committee.

7.   Increase the AU Commission budget to enable the Commission to prepare effectively for summits and other AU processes.

8.   In the absence of additional financing to the Commission, consider reducing, at least in the short term, the number of meetings of the AU Assembly of Heads of State and Government to once a year, with scheduled meetings of the Permanent Representatives Committee and Executive Council of Ministers twice a year as currently. Reduce the number of extraordinary summits.

9.   Require any country hosting a summit to commit in advance (at the time the offer to host the summit is made) to facilitate civil society access. This should include easy granting of visas, freedom from harassment for civil society representatives, facilitation where necessary for civil society meetings and ensuring that adequate accommodation is available for delegates from civil society as well as government. The AU Commission should include these requirements in the agreement signed with the host country.

10.   Amend the rules of procedure of the Executive Council of Ministers and the Assembly to require all meetings whose deliberations and resolutions will be considered at a summit to be held at least six weeks before the summit. This should enable reports of meetings to be translated and circulated in good time.

11.   Establish and publish a calendar for AU meetings at the outset of each year. This calendar should indicate deadlines for documents to be received in respect of each meeting.

12.   Respect the rules of procedure of the Executive Council of Ministers and Assembly of Heads of State and Government. In particular, if member states do not submit proposed agenda items on time and with appropriate documentation the items should not be listed on the summit agendas for discussion. A separate procedure could be specified for exceptional situations where the rule may be waived.

13.   Ensure that draft decisions considered at summits are thoroughly debated and properly prepared before they are presented to the Executive Council and Assembly. This should lead to smoother functioning of the decision-making process.

14.   Establish and respect official hours of work for summit meetings. There should be time limits for debates on individual agenda items and member state contributions to the debates.

15.   Make use of the rules of procedure that enable the PRC to form committees and hear briefings from civil society organisations in relation to any topic in which their expertise may be useful.

16.   Review and clarify the role of regional economic communities at summits. As already recognised, the various RECs should be rationalised, and a mechanism should be devised to enable a meaningful role during summits. In principle, the regional blocs organised within the PRC and the RECs should be congruent, in order to make the regional decision-making processes more transparent.

The AU Commission

Government officials interviewed for this report cited the late distribution of documents in advance of summits as a key problem affecting their participation in decision-making. Civil society organisations find it far more difficult to obtain information about what will be discussed at upcoming AU meetings. The Commission should exercise the considerable autonomy it has under the Constitutive Act to find alternative and more efficient ways of enabling public access to information.

The pre-summit civil society and women's forums organised by the AU Commission could become important spaces to inform participants, listen to their views and build continental consensus on priorities and issues to be discussed during the summits. However, procedures for selection and accreditation of participants are unclear. The quality of debate at the main civil society forum is often poor and insufficiently linked to the Assembly agenda; though in recent years, the women's forum has tended to be more open and more strategic in its interaction with the summit debates. There is a need to learn from these early experiences, both to strengthen these meetings and to define the best ways for them to interact with the newly established ECOSOCC.

Since 2004, the Women, Gender and Development Directorate at the AU Commission has led the way in working with civil society organisations. This openness and the strength of women's rights organisations' advocacy is reflected in the AU's adoption of the Solemn Declaration on Gender Equality in Africa, as well as the entry into force in record time of the Protocol on the Rights of Women in Africa to the African Charter on Human and Peoples' Rights. The African Citizens' Directorate (CIDO) of the AU Commission, charged with the main responsibility to facilitate civil society engagement with the AU organs and processes, has also assisted civil society participation at AU summits. However, current capacity in both institutions and in other directorates is insufficient to ensure that the AU Commission engages seriously with civil society on each of the policy areas in which it is working.

To remedy these defects perhaps the most urgent requirement is for mechanisms to improve access to and distribution of information about AU processes, both for member states and civil society organisations. In addition, the AU Commission's interaction with civil society organisations should be more transparent and more open to a wider range of groups.

Recommendations for the AU Commission

The African Union Commission should:

17.   Prepare a policy on information disclosure and access for adoption by the PRC, modelled on international best practice. This policy should provide for automatic publication of most documents, as well as the right for African citizens to request and obtain access to all official documents, except where explicitly categorised as confidential according to published, restrictive criteria. Denial of access should be subject to an appeal procedure.

18.   Seek and invest more substantial resources for the rapid translation and distribution of documents needed for summits and other meetings. This should include exploring new media technologies that could allow for papers to be downloaded directly by state officials in their capital cities, thus circumventing the need for the embassy in Addis Ababa to pass on the documentation manually.

19.   Adequately resource and improve the AU website, in particular to keep all details up to date, provide a search function and archive system and complete those sections that are currently empty.

20.   At minimum, publish on the AU website the draft agendas for summit meetings and supporting documents (including the AU Commission Chairperson's report on activities and documents submitted on agenda items by states) as soon as they are distributed to states.

21.   Ensure that an accurate record of the proceedings of each summit is prepared and circulated within one month of the summit to all accredited participants and made available on the AU website.

22.   Initiate consultations on revised criteria for observer status for civil society organisations at the AU that would increase the number of qualifying organisations.

23.   Adopt clear criteria to govern and advertise the process by which civil society organisations may obtain support from the AU Commission for their accreditation to attend AU summits.

24.   Instruct all departments to consult as widely as possible with non-state actors in the development of decisions to be adopted at summits, including civil society organisations and representatives of those people directly affected by the issues being discussed.

25.   Clarify and publicise the different functions of CIDO and ECOSOCC. CIDO should be required and given the resources to enable it to respond promptly to all inquiries about AU procedures and processes.

26.   CIDO and the Women, Gender and Development Directorate should establish a steering committee to draw up the programmes for their respective pre-summit forums, publicly announce the meetings, invite papers and presentations on the summit themes and solicit interest in participation. The composition of the steering committee should rotate among organisations to ensure there is no 'AU capture' by a small set of insiders. The role of ECOSOCC in these fora should be clarified.

27.   Compile a database of all NGO coalitions and networks in Africa, especially those that are engaged in key issues for the AU. Where the lead organisations are apparent on a particular issue, the AU Commission should send papers to the relevant organisation(s) with the requirement that they in turn distribute the documents further. These organisations should be listed on the AU Commission website.

ECOSOCC

The research for this report found a general welcome for the establishment of ECOSOCC. However, key policy and institutional obstacles constrain its ability to deliver on the promise of a civil society voice within the AU. First, the structures of ECOSOCC are not sufficiently supported at the continental level. The Interim Standing Committee of ECOSOCC remains too reliant on the African Citizen's Directorate for funding, advice and administrative support. Secondly, the processes for election of ECOSOCC national chapters and continental representatives are unclear and flawed, while eligibility criteria established by the ECOSOCC Statutes exclude many civil society organisations with a contribution to make. Thirdly, despite sub-regional and national consultations, there is need to increase publicity and knowledge of ECOSOCC. A number of national chapters are yet to be activated or are poorly functioning. Finally, ECOSOCC's legal framework as an organ with only advisory status, and without its own treaty, significantly weakens its position. For these reasons, as currently constituted, ECOSOCC is unable to speak credibly as an independent civil society voice. If the ECOSOCC and civil society leadership are able to break through these obstacles, ECOSOCC has the potential eventually to become a genuine voice for Africa's citizens within the AU system.

The report also considers organised civil society interaction with two African inter-governmental bodies at the regional level: the Southern Africa Development Community (SADC) and the Economic Community of West African States (ECOWAS). The West African Civil Society Forum, in particular, is a useful model: it is not an organ of ECOWAS but an autonomous structure with its own sources of funding. ECOSOCC could and should learn lessons from these experiences.

If ECOSOCC is to play the role intended for it, it must become a much more genuinely representative body; this will require both significant strengthening of the processes for electing representatives to its structures and a stronger position for ECOSOCC itself within the AU organs.

Recommendations for ECOSOCC

28. The ECOSOCC Interim Steering Committee should initiate a widely consultative planning process to take into account recommendations in this report and elsewhere relating to the future role and function of ECOSOCC.

29. The ECOSOCC Interim Steering Committee should provide procedural guidelines and secure adequate resources for the election of final ECOSOCC structures at national and continental level. These elections should be as transparent and democratic as possible.

30. The rules of procedure of the PRC, Executive Council and Assembly, and the ECOSOCC Statutes, should be amended to require ECOSOCC to be consulted prior to draft decisions being forwarded to heads of state by the PRC or Executive Council.

31. The public profile and role of ECOSOCC national chapters in relation to information distribution should be strengthened. The AU Commission could be required to distribute all documents relevant to AU summits directly to the ECOSOCC national chapters at the same time as they are distributed to states. The ECOSOCC national chapter could then distribute the documents to all national civil society organisations registered with it and convene a meeting in advance of each summit. In this meeting, foreign affairs ministries could brief civil society organisations and seek their opinions on draft government positions. The ECOSOCC national chapters should conduct awareness campaigns about their role.

32. The ECOSOCC Interim Steering Committee should publicise its role and purpose through active leadership and participation in the AU-CSO Forum and other civil society meetings.

33. The ECOSOCC Assembly should meet during the time of the AU summits and in the same location. Its agenda should relate closely to the summit debates. In this way it would promote interaction between the AU's civil society body and state representatives.

Civil society

Civil society organisations are playing an increasingly visible role in engaging directly with the AU Commission – outside the ECOSOCC framework – around a diverse set of policy issues, including HIV/AIDS, women's rights, debt, trade, human rights and the culture of impunity. Space for this autonomous, direct civil society interaction with the AU will remain of critical importance to promote the ability of civil society to contribute to the AU.

Recommendations to civil society organisations

34. Widely distribute information about the AU and adapt it to different audiences, including the media, academia, parliaments, and schools. Civil society organisations have a responsibility to ensure that the message of African unity is popularised to the widest extent.

35. Increase coordination around autonomous interaction with AU summits and make greater efforts to transmit civil society conclusions and recommendations to official summit participants. This will

increase the effectiveness of civil society advocacy and help to ensure a genuine dialogue between Africa's citizens and leaders.

36.   Mobilise resources and support for current initiatives to establish independent civil society offices and facilities in Ethiopia and South Africa to facilitate access for African citizens to AU institutions and disseminate information about the AU processes as widely as possible.

2. BACKGROUND: THE AFRICAN UNION

African states created the African Union (AU) in the new millennium[1] to replace the Organisation of African Unity (OAU), in existence since 1963. The OAU was set up among other things to defend the sovereignty, territorial integrity and independence of African states and to eradicate all forms of colonialism from Africa.[2] The AU, by contrast, has the ambition to create 'a united and integrated Africa; an Africa imbued with justice and peace; an interdependent and robust Africa determined to map for itself an ambitious strategy; an Africa underpinned by political, economic, social and cultural integration which would restore to Pan-Africanism its full meaning'[3] and composed only of 'democratic states respectful of human rights and keen to build equitable societies'.[4]

The African Union requires each of its member states to 'promote and protect human and peoples' rights, consolidate democratic institutions and culture, and ... ensure good governance and the rule of law';[5] promote peace, security and stability on the continent;[6] and found its actions on essential principles such as respect for the sanctity of human life, promotion of equality between men and women, and condemnation of impunity and unconstitutional changes of government.[7] The principle of non-interference in internal affairs was replaced by a principle of non-indifference to the problems facing African states and 'the right of the Union to intervene in a member state pursuant to a decision of the Assembly in respect of grave circumstances, namely war crimes, genocide and crimes against humanity'[8] as well as to impose sanctions on states failing to comply with the policies and decisions of the Union.[9] Governments coming to power through unconstitutional means are not allowed to participate in the activities of the Union,[10] and the Union is required to 'promote democratic principles and institutions, popular participation and good governance'.[11]

The adoption by the AU of the New Partnership for Africa's Development (NEPAD) and the African Peer Review Mechanism (APRM), designed to review African states' compliance with continental treaties and other standards, was a further mark of a new commitment by member states to respect for good governance, human rights and the rule of law.

This new vision was implemented at the institutional level by the creation of new organs, as set out in the Constitutive Act of the AU. The principal decision-making body remains the Assembly of Heads of State and Government, supported by the Executive Council of Ministers (made up of ministers of foreign affairs) and the Permanent Representatives Committee (which comprises the ambassadors accredited to the AU Commission in Addis Ababa). The OAU Secretariat was transformed into the AU Commission, headed by a chairperson, deputy chairperson, and eight commissioners appointed by member states, and substantially re-organised into new departments.[12] Two new institutions – the Pan-African Parliament and the Economic, Social and Cultural Council (ECOSOCC) – were designed specifically to increase the voice of Africa's peoples in the AU's decision-making procedures. Other institutions which have yet to be set up are the Court of Justice, financial institutions, and specialised technical committees responsible to the Executive Council.[13] A protocol to the Constitutive Act providing for the establishment of a Peace and Security Council was adopted in Durban in July 2002.[14]

The responsibilities of the president of the continental body, elected from among their number by heads of state and government at the January session of the Assembly, also increased with the creation of the African Union. The president can now expect to be heavily involved in conflict resolution and other activities of the continental body. Since 2002, the rotational system of annual hosting and chairing of summits has passed through South Africa, Mozambique and Nigeria, and in 2006 arrived at the doorstep of Congo Brazzaville (see further below, on the decision on the presidency of the African Union). The country that holds the presidency of the Union also, during the same period, chairs the sessions of the Executive Council[15] and the Permanent Representatives Committee[16] of the African Union.

Documents adopted by the OAU, including the treaty establishing the African Economic Community[17] and the African Charter for Popular Participation in Development,[18] already recognised the important role of civil society in the work of continental integration – though the challenge was always to transform these commitments into reality. The African Union makes much more significant commitments, including to 'build a partnership between governments and all segments of civil society, in particular women, youth and the private sector, in order to strengthen solidarity and cohesion among our peoples',[19] and to make Africans 'both the actors in and beneficiaries of the structural changes engendered by development'.[20] The Commission notes that:

> The decision to establish the African Parliament and the Economic, Social and Cultural Council (ECOSOCC), and to organise Pan-African integration associations, particularly women's and youth associations, in the spirit of pluralism and respect for differences, and other civil society organisations should leave no one in any doubt about the commitment of African Heads of State to give concrete meaning to participation and partnership, and their will to make the African Union a tool to build a new equilibrium between state and non-state actors on solid foundations, a prerequisite for meaningful people's ownership of and participation in the integration process.[21]

Since it was established the AU Commission has worked to put into practice the objectives of the Union. For this purpose, the first chair of the Commission, Alpha Oumar Konaré, former president of Mali, led a process of wide consultation leading to the drafting and adoption of a strategic plan, vision and mission for the AU Commission. The strategic plan for 2004–2007 set out five 'priority programmes', of which the second was to 'actively involve African citizens at large and members of the diaspora in the process of building continental integration'.[22]

The AU Commission has a staff complement of between 400 and 500, which, it contends, is inadequate to deal effectively with the new work being generated by the wider mandate of the AU compared to the OAU and the demands of member states: the AU Commission has to respond to the needs of twice as many countries as the European Union Commission with a fiftieth of the staff.[23] Member states did not approve the proposed AU Commission budget of US$570 million for 2005; instead, only slightly over 25 per cent (US$158.4 million) was approved.[24] Of this amount, assessed member state contributions support the core operating costs of the Commission of US$63 million, while support for programmatic activities comes from voluntary contributions, by both member states and external donors. Of the assessed contributions of member states, 15 per cent of the budget is paid by each of Algeria, Egypt, Libya, Nigeria and South Africa.[25] Major donors to the AU Commission include the European Union.[26]

A new management team for the AU Commission – chairperson, deputy and commissioners – will be elected at the AU summit to be held in Accra, Ghana, in July 2007. In the meantime, on the agenda for consideration at the January 2007 summit to be held in Addis Ababa is an ambitious proposal for the creation of a Union government, which would completely restructure the AU institutions.[27]

3. PREPARATION OF AU SUMMITS AT CONTINENTAL LEVEL

The AU holds two summits a year: in January and June/July. Ordinarily, the January summit is held in Addis Ababa, Ethiopia (the headquarters of the AU Commission), and the June/July summit rotates.[28] Member states have made offers to host the July summits of the AU up to 2012. The decision to hold two summits, taken at the June 2004 summit,[29] was intended to allow the first to attend to policy and strategic planning and the second to focus on the budget and operational matters.[30] In practice, having two summits allows for those issues that were not discussed at the first to be covered at the next summit.[31] In addition, the heads of state and government have quite often called an extraordinary summit on a specific theme during the inter-summit period. In 2006, for example, there was a 'special summit' on malaria, tuberculosis, and HIV/AIDS in Abuja, Nigeria, 1–4 May 2006, and an extraordinary meeting of the Executive Council on African Union government also held in Abuja, Nigeria, 17–18 November 2006.

The decision to hold two summits a year appears to have created significant difficulties for the AU Commission, since the schedule does not allow sufficient time to implement decisions before the preparation begins for the next summit. Representatives of the PRC and AU Commission interviewed for this report were unanimous that the decision to hold two summits a year had negative consequences for the efficiency of implementation of the AU's work programme.[32]

In addition to preparing for the summits themselves, the AU Commission has to provide support for numerous other ministerial, PRC or experts' meetings held during the inter-summit period to inform summit decisions or other work of the AU. There can be more than 100 such meetings in any six-month period, putting a significant strain on the human and financial resources available.

The Rules of Procedure of the Executive Council of Ministers and of the Assembly of Heads of State and Government provide a framework for the preparation of and procedures at summits.[33] In addition, the Statutes of the Commission of the AU (2002) outline the role of the AU Commission in the preparation of summits.[34]

The key institutions in the preparation of summits include the PRC, the Office of the Chairperson of the AU Commission and the conferencing department in the AU Commission. The Offices of the Chairperson and Deputy Chairperson and the Conferencing and Events Department of the AU Commission are responsible for the managing the process of preparing for summits.[35]

There are two aspects to the preparation of meetings: the logistics at the proposed location and the substantive issues to be discussed. At the end of one summit, a bureau is established to begin preparations on both logistical and substantive issues for the next summit. The 15-member bureau, which comprises the president of the AU and representatives of member states elected by the PRC, will direct logistical preparations and compile a provisional agenda.

On logistics, the AU Commission, through the Office of the Chairperson, will make the initial contact with the host country. A month after the previous summit, an appraisal team, normally led by the deputy chairperson, will conduct a visit at the proposed location for the summit. The team consists of representatives from the departments of protocol, security, communications, administration and finance, and conferencing. After the visit, the team will report back to the chairperson of the AU. An agreement will be signed between the AU Commission and the hosting government which includes requirements in relation to accommodation, logistical support, size of meeting rooms, and other matters. However, given that the Assembly will approve the location of a summit long before the host agreement is signed, it is in practice difficult for the Commission to enforce these requirements in the case of small countries that have limited resources.

On substantive issues there are two sources of input to the agenda, described below: the activities of the various commissioners and their departments or other AU organs, and member states. Commissioners are invited to submit their agenda items and a list of people they wish to invite to the summit; member states may submit their own agenda items.

Preparation of the agenda

The agenda for an ordinary session of the Assembly of the African Union is, in principle, established by the Executive Council.[36] However, in practice, this task is carried out by the PRC.[37]

The draft agenda necessarily includes:[38]
- the report of the AU Commission;
- the report of the PRC;
- the items the Assembly of the Union has submitted to the Executive Council;
- the items that the Executive Council has decided, during a previous session, to include on the agenda;
- the draft programme budget of the Union;
- the items proposed by the other organs of the Union;
- the items proposed by the member states;
- other business proposed by the organs of the Union, the regional economic communities or the member states.[39]

The agenda of the main policy-making organs – the Assembly of Heads of State and Government and the Executive Council of Ministers of the AU – is structured in the following manner:
- Administrative and financial matters;
- Legal, political and institutional matters;
- Economic, social and cultural matters;
- Implementation report by the AU chair on the extent of implementation of decisions taken at the previous summit;
- Agenda items proposed by member states.[40]

The AU Commission is the source of many agenda items at the summit, based on the sectoral expert meetings which take place between summits and prepare draft documents for adoption by the Assembly or Executive Council. These sectoral meetings have no formal basis in the AU legal framework, but are convened by the various commissioners or directorates under the authority of the Executive Council. In general, they are attended by government-appointed experts, but civil society organisations may also be invited to attend where they have special expertise, and they can be important opportunities for civil society input to the AU agenda items; the practice in this regard varies across the various Commission directorates. Once the

Executive Council adopts a draft coming from a sectoral meeting, the Office of the Legal Counsel in the AU Commission will draft a decision for adoption by the Assembly at the summit.

Preparatory documents are supposed to be distributed well in advance of these meetings to member states, through their representatives in Addis Ababa. However, this is often not the case. One member of the PRC described the current system for distribution and discussion of documents at expert meetings as 'catastrophic', noting that the text of the draft Charter on Democracy, Elections and Governance – a document of major importance to the AU agenda – had reached the embassy in Addis Ababa only two days before an experts' meeting at which it was to be discussed, leaving no time for consultation with his capital.[41]

Other agenda items come from other AU organs, such as the consideration of the annual activity report of the African Commission on Human and Peoples' Rights or, at recent summits, the report of the interim president of ECOSOCC.

Items proposed by the member states must be submitted to the chair of the AU Commission at least two months before the summit, while related documents and draft decisions may be submitted only one month in advance.[42] In practice, member states intending to propose agenda items frequently do not observe the time limits; yet the proposed items are invariably accepted for debate.[43] The states may also raise additional questions at any time, but these questions may not form the basis of a debate or decision.[44]

During 2006, several of the countries considered for this report proposed the introduction of items on the agenda of one of the two summits:
- 'Migration and Development'[45] by Algeria for the Khartoum summit;
- 'Rethinking the Commission on Labour and Social Affairs'[46] by Congo for the Banjul summit;
- 'Report on the 23rd Summit of Heads of State and Government of France and Africa'[47] and 'The creation of an African Research Centre on Migration'[48] by Mali for the Khartoum and Banjul summits respectively;
- 'The Hissène Habré case and the African Union' by Senegal for the Khartoum summit;
- 'International Day of African Football' by Ethiopia for the Khartoum summit;[49]
- 'Consideration of the Memorandum of the United Cities and Local Government of Africa (UCGLA) to the African Union' by South Africa for the Khartoum summit.[50]

Once the Assembly has been formally opened, the provisional draft agenda is submitted to the delegates for adoption. The version presented to them at that time includes two parts:[51]
- Part A, comprising the items approved by the Executive Council, which will be submitted to the Assembly for adoption without debate;
- Part B, including all items on which a consensus was not reached within the Executive Council, and which need to be debated prior to their approval by the Assembly.

Distribution of documents to member states

It is the responsibility of the chairperson of the AU Commission to distribute the draft agenda to member states.[52] Under Rule 9(2) of the Rules of Procedure of the Executive Council of Ministers, the chairperson shall send a provisional agenda to member states through their representatives in Addis Ababa at least thirty days before the summit.[53] The note is transmitted to capitals for action; thus the diplomatic missions in Addis Ababa play an important role in obtaining documents as soon as they are ready. The AU Commission should also distribute all supporting documentation, including the reports of ministerial meetings, legal experts meeting and draft decisions. The Indian government is assisting the Commission in developing information technology tools for the distribution of documents.

A concern raised by national and regional officials interviewed is that although the provisional agenda is more often reaching them in time than in the past, other documents reach them too late for adequate preparation. The AU Commission has acknowledged this difficulty, which is in part due to meetings taking place too close to the summit. In preparation for the Banjul 2006 summit, all reports were due to be submitted to the AU Commission by 15 May,[54] yet some preparatory meetings ended after the closing date for the submission of reports – such as the meeting on the integration of the African Court on Human and Peoples' Rights and the Court of Justice of the AU, which took place on 16–19 May.

The agenda items submitted by member states create similar problems for the AU Commission. One of the documents prepared by Mali for the Banjul summit was dated 1 June 2006,[55] whereas the session of the Executive Council during which the paper was reviewed commenced on 25 June 2006.[56] Supporting documentation to the agenda item raised by the government of Senegal on the Hissène Habré matter did not reach all member states before the Khartoum summit; some states had to do their own research in order to have sufficient information to formulate an opinion.[57] Libya proposed more than one agenda item at each of the last four summits and, during a visit to the AU Commission in mid-May 2006, submitted a proposal for the agenda on 'Legislation for Organising and Ensuring Respect for Social Life in Africa' without any supporting documentation. Cameroon, however, had submitted an agenda item with supporting documentation in French and English on 'Transformation of the All-Africa Ministerial Conference on Decentralisation and Local Development to an African Union Structure'.[58] The papers are often submitted in skeleton form[59] and are not very informative,[60] although the supporting documents may be voluminous.[61]

Further delay is produced by the requirement that documents can only be distributed once available in all four official languages of the AU (Arabic, English, French and Portuguese); thus, while the AU would ideally prefer sending all documents in a single batch, this does not always occur.[62]

Documents can reach member states as late as a week before the summit. According to the Botswana Foreign Ministry, documents on the report of the AU Commission on the Strategic Framework for Migration Policy[63] reached the ministry only a week before the Banjul summit, which meant that the ministry was unable to request comments from the government agencies responsible for labour and internal affairs.[64] For Mozambique, the Foreign Affairs Ministry drew on a memo written by its embassy in Addis Ababa to assist with the formulation of positions for the Banjul summit, given the late receipt of the draft agenda.[65]

These delays create numerous problems for summit decision-making: because of the little time for consultation, member states may not have reached advance consensus on a document, so that negotiations on the text may need to continue in depth at the summit itself. As a result, the final text may suffer from poor quality drafting or differences of meaning among the various language versions.

The role of the Permanent Representatives Committee

The PRC is perhaps the most important AU institution in the preparation of decisions that will be adopted at AU summits: it is where the political deals are made that turn technical drafting into formal policy. However, member states' permanent representatives in Addis Ababa do not only prepare for summits; they are critical players in bringing the AU agenda into the day to day reality of government business in capital cities around the continent. The permanent representatives in Addis Ababa are engaged in a variety of deal-making that is not directly linked to summits, as well as formally taking part in the PRC meetings.

The PRC is supposed to meet at least once a month to discuss recommendations for adoption by the Executive Council; in practice, because of the pressure of other meetings, this schedule is not always followed. The PRC rules of procedure allow it to form any sub-committees it wishes and to collect information from any source;

including civil society organisations, if desired. Current sub-committees include the following: administration, finance and budgetary affairs; Africa/EU dialogue; multi lateral relations; trade and economic affairs; refugees, migration and internally displaced persons; AU structures; and calendar of events.

Building consensus by region

Decision-making at the AU is premised on consensus. In Addis Ababa, regular consultations take place at ambassadorial level, where member states arrange themselves according the five regions: east, west, north, central and southern Africa.[66] Each region elects a 'dean' who convenes meetings of the ambassadors in Addis Ababa, and also in the margins of the AU summits, to determine a common position of the region on AU issues. The southern and west African regions are perhaps the most coherent of these groups; the most important countries in each sub-region, South Africa and Nigeria, play an essential role. The southern region (which does not mirror the REC configuration, as it excludes the Democratic Republic of the Congo, Mauritius and Tanzania) meets at least once a month in Addis. Member states will reach a common position on most issues: for example, on the election of judges to the African Court on Human and Peoples' Rights, member states from the southern region voted for candidates from their region.[67] Similarly, west African states meet on a monthly basis in Addis Ababa, as well as during the summits: the regional representatives met three times during the Khartoum summit before deciding to oppose any attempt by Sudan to be chair of the AU. By contrast, the north African region failed to adopt a common position on Sudan's candidacy.

Consultations at REC level – for example at heads of state or ministerial meetings of SADC or ECOWAS – provide further opportunities for consensus building (though the fact that the political regions do not mirror the RECs provides space for confusion). For example, the SADC Assembly of Heads of State and Government met in October 2006 to discuss the issue of rationalisation of RECs and the Union of African States in preparation for the November 2006 extraordinary meeting of the Executive Council and the January 2007 AU summit. ECOWAS holds ministerial meetings immediately before AU summits, giving opportunities to west African states to share their views; the ECOWAS executive secretary may also participate in these meetings. If a summit theme has particular importance for ECOWAS, national ambassadors in Abuja will form part of the state delegation to the AU summit. Representatives of other intergovernmental organisations accredited to the African Union, such as the *Organisation Internationale de la Francophonie*, may also be consulted.

Conduct of the summit

The management of AU summits varies according to the country in which they are held: summits held in Addis Ababa, the headquarters of the Union, are obviously easier to manage for AU Commission staff. Summits held in wealthier member states (such as South Africa) also inevitably tend to run more smoothly in relation to logistical matters than in less well-resourced countries. In some cases (including both Khartoum and Banjul during 2006), there are often acute shortages of accommodation, or even seating space in the meeting rooms.

In some respects, however, poor management of summit meetings is unconnected to logistical issues. In particular, there is little or no discipline over the speaking time of delegates nor the working hours of the meeting: in both 2006 summits the Executive Council and Assembly meetings went on to the early hours of the morning, only to reconvene at the usual time the next morning. Consequently, decisions may be impossible to take for lack of quorum, or delegates who choose to sleep may be excluded from debates.

Most sessions of the Assembly are closed, meaning that only official delegations can attend; however, some are open and form an important opportunity for information gathering by civil society organisations and others (see further below). These include the opening of the Executive Council and Assembly and some other deliberative sessions, at which civil society groups may observe but not speak. The PRC meetings are formally closed to civil society groups, though the RECs and United Nations (UN) organs may observe them.

The rules of procedure for the meetings held at the summit are currently under review, providing an opportunity to address some of the problems with efficient running of the AU's business.

Follow-up to summit decisions

Each summit meeting includes an agenda item on implementation of previous decisions, on which a report is presented by the chair of the AU Commission. However, beyond this report, which is not made public for African citizens to be informed of the effectiveness of their continental body, there is no formal process of ensuring implementation of decisions by the AU organs; indeed, several informed insiders suggested that decisions of the AU Assembly were often adopted in the full knowledge that they are not implementable. There is a proposal to establish a committee of the PRC on implementation of summit decisions, which would be a welcome initiative; the AU Commission departments are also supposed to monitor implementation of decisions, but this is not currently happening.[68]

Unlike earlier documents, several important new African treaties have no formal enforcement mechanism to ensure that their commitments are respected, raising the risk that they will remain simply aspirational statements with no real force. For example, the African Commission on Human and Peoples' Rights and the Committee of Experts on the Rights and Welfare of the Child the are responsible for ensuring respect for the African Charter on Human and Peoples' Rights (adopted 1981) and the African Charter on the Rights and Welfare of the Child (1990), respectively. However, the Convention on Preventing and Combating Corruption (2003), for example, has no similar body; nor has the proposed Charter on Democracy Elections and Governance (to be debated at the January 2007 summit of the AU).

Although decisions and recommendations of the Executive Council and Assembly are made public on the AU website, related documents are often not included, without which the decision is meaningless and hard to monitor. For example, the 20th Annual Activity report of the African Commission on Human and Peoples' Rights, adopted (with qualifications) by the Executive Council at Banjul in July 2006, is not available on either commission's website, even though it is supposed to be publicly available once the summit has approved it and was indeed available at the summit itself. It is quite common for decisions of the Assembly or Executive Council to be in the form that the organ: 'takes note of the report on [a particular topic] and adopts the recommendations therein', with no further details available.

Historically, the AU Commission has prepared a record of proceedings of meetings at AU summits; however, since the decision to hold two summits a year this has not happened consistently, due to lack of capacity. This in itself makes it much more difficult to follow the reasoning behind the decisions made and ensure effective implementation.

4. PREPARATIONS FOR SUMMITS BY MEMBER STATES

The quality of preparation for the meetings of the Executive Council of Ministers and Assembly of Heads of State and Government differs from state to state. An observer of AU summits remarked that over half of the member states do not prepare adequately.[69]

Those member states that prepare well for summits fall into two categories: the pace-setters, which are progressive in outlook, readily embrace democratic principles and support the integration agenda and those that respond cautiously to issues of democracy, placing an emphasis on state sovereignty.[70] These member states will prepare positions on all agenda items and tend to meet their financial contributions to the AU.[71] They include those contributing 15 per cent each to the AU budget (Algeria, Egypt, Libya, Nigeria and South Africa), who have thus invested in the success of the institution, but also some smaller countries, especially in southern Africa, who place importance on AU decision-making processes and their obligations to participate. The reasons for this differing level of engagement are varied, and would merit further research: some states appear to place more importance on United Nations summits and processes than the AU equivalents; others on engagement with their respective sub-regional bodies; some simply seem to place less value on the obligations that membership of an organisation implies.

A further factor in the ability of member states to prepare sufficiently for summits is the capacity of government agencies to undertake the work. Thus, for instance, Algeria has an entire 'Africa Branch', which includes a multilateral relations section that heads a unit specifically responsible for the African Union;[72] while in Mali, the African Union falls within the scope of the Africa division of the Political Affairs Branch. In Mozambique, though, the AU and Multi-lateral Department responsible for summit preparations has only three officials, and prior to July 2006 had only one person. In the bigger countries, the foreign affairs ministry will most likely have a legal affairs division; for example, South Africa and Ethiopia and all the francophone countries studied. In Botswana, by contrast, the Foreign Affairs Ministry does not have a legal affairs unit; these issues are the preserve of the Attorney General's chambers.

The capacity of the embassy in Addis Ababa is also critical. Many embassies in Addis Ababa are under-staffed, meaning that briefings on meetings that the permanent representatives attend may not be rapidly transmitted back to their respective foreign ministries and other relevant government departments. The simple addition of a member of staff with this responsibility in all embassies in Addis Ababa could be a useful contribution to more effective and consultative decision-making at the AU level.

National structures responsible for foreign affairs

In the civil law countries in Africa, the structure and responsibility of government officials is founded on a constitutional and regulatory legal framework that clearly defines their operational responsibilities. Their constitutions proclaim the attachment of their populations and national institutions to the ideals of the African Union and grant the executive the legal means to make this ideal a concrete reality.[73] This explicit constitutional commitment to African unity is generally not present to the same extent in the Commonwealth countries.

The constitutions of the civil law countries also grant substantial powers to the president of the republic in matters of foreign policy,[74] including the responsibility to appoint ministers and ambassadors and negotiate international commitments. Thus, in general, the staff of the office of the president includes at least one diplomatic adviser in charge of African affairs,[75] a chief of protocol, and a representative/attaché.

Similarly, the constitutions provide for the position of prime minister, whose role is to implement policy defined by the president,[76] and to act as a go-between or interface between the president and other organs of the state. Under certain circumstances, the prime minister may also represent the president at summits and thus take a direct role in decision-making.[77] Where this is the case, the office of the prime minister must include a diplomatic adviser working in coordination with his counterparts in the office of the president and with the departments concerned at the ministry of foreign affairs and other ministries interested in the agenda of the African Union summits. The prime minister also plays an important role in the preparation and conduct of the inter-ministerial consultations that are often organised in the context of preparations for and follow up to African Union summits.

Only Algeria and Republic of Congo, among the civil law countries studied for this report, had updated the decrees regulating conduct of foreign affairs to reflect the transformation of the OAU into the AU.[78] The other countries are thus forced to improvise solutions to respond to the new structures.

In common law countries, the specific responsibilities for conduct of foreign affairs are not set out in the constitution and law in the same way. However, the president will always play an important role in setting foreign policy, even if this is not written down explicitly. Most African Commonwealth countries no longer have a post of prime minister, but where one exists the prime minister is the head of government, with responsibility for government policy in general, including foreign policy, and the presidency is a ceremonial post.[79]

The minister of foreign affairs plays a very similar role in all countries studied, leading the process of preparation for summits; with the difference that in the civil law countries this role is spelt out in written decrees.[80] The ministry will then include specific units or departments that may be relevant to AU summits, including in particular units in charge of relations with the African Union, legal affairs, political affairs and international organisations or multilateral relations in general.

In several countries there are specific additional or subordinate ministries (ministres délégués) with responsibilities that mean they are always also closely involved in summit preparations. For example, in Algeria, there is a minister in charge of Maghrebian and African Affairs;[81] in Mali, there is a Ministry of Malians Abroad and African Integration;[82] and in Senegal, a Ministry for NEPAD, African Economic Integration and Good Governance Policy. Kenya and other east African countries have ministries for regional integration. The justice department, in particular the international affairs section, is also consulted in most instances for comments, as there is invariably an agenda item on legal matters.

The ambassadors appointed by member states to the African Union also play a key role in summit preparations. In most cases, the diplomatic missions to Ethiopia also fulfil the functions of diplomatic representation to the African Union and the United Nations Economic Commission for Africa (ECA), whose headquarters are located in the Ethiopian capital. In the case of some of the civil law countries, the relevant decrees give these ambassadors, in addition to their usual roles, specific responsibilities to assist non-governmental institutions in their relations with foreign partners.[83] In addition, those countries that have their nationals in key positions within the AU Commission draw on them for information and advice about strategy in AU decision-making.

The sequence of events in the preparation for AU summits in civil law countries is usually as follows, with small variations.

- The ministry of foreign affairs receives the agenda from its mission in Addis Ababa, and immediately organises, through its African Union branch, an internal consultation that is generally attended by the legal affairs branch, the international organisations branch and, according to the importance of the summit, the general secretariat of the ministry and the office of the minister. The aim of this initial consultation is to provide the ministry with a more complete vision of the issues to be discussed during the summit.
- At the outcome of the consultation, a document is produced and presented to the minister. It contains the comments and suggestions made by the ambassador in Addis Ababa at the time of sending of the agenda.
- Following that, the ministry of foreign affairs dispatches the various technical documents to the technical ministries covering the proposed topics for their written comments.
- An inter-ministerial consultation is then organised by the ministry of foreign affairs, in close collaboration with the office of the president of the republic and the concerned departments of the office of the prime minister, with a view to preparing a fact sheet for each item on the agenda and ensuring that the other ministries cover all the technical aspects of the items on the summit agenda.
- At the outcome of these two consultations, the fact sheets are gathered into a single file containing the draft position papers on each agenda item or, at least, on the items of particular interest to the country in question. The file is presented to the minister for approval.
- After such approval is obtained, it is submitted to the president of the republic who provides a clear political orientation on each of the proposals contained in the file. (It may happen that the president gives instructions that are in total contradiction with the proposals put forward by the consultations organised under the aegis of the ministry of foreign affairs.)
- While the file is being prepared, the ministry remains in regular contact with the ambassador accredited to Addis Ababa for updates on the items on the agenda and opinions on the proposed positions.
- After it is prepared, the document is presented to the president for approval. The president submits it to his staff for an in-depth review, following which it is formally approved.

In common law countries, the process is not dissimilar:

- Officials at the diplomatic mission in Addis Ababa transmit documents to the department of foreign affairs. The documents will be accompanied by a briefing document from the ambassador in Addis Ababa who also sits on the PRC. This briefing document contains observations on positions of other member states on particular issues on the agenda.
- At the department of foreign affairs, the document is referred to the relevant official who heads the AU/Africa affairs desk. The Africa affairs desk may comprise a team of six officers. They will be responsible for drafting the briefs.
- A director within the foreign affairs department holds a meeting within the department to chart a strategy. This includes identification of relevant departments to make inputs under the agenda items.

- Depending on the issues, lead government agencies such as the department of justice/attorney general's office will be requested to submit the government's position on the relevant agenda item. The AU Department will give the governments agencies requested to make submissions a period by which inputs should be receive.
- An inter-departmental meeting is held to discuss the submissions. The permanent secretary (or deputy) of the ministry of foreign affairs or director general/director within the department of foreign affairs will lead these meetings.
- On an ad-hoc basis, the officials at the AU/Africa desk may meet with civil society to discuss specific issues that may be discussed at the summit.
- The AU/Africa desk coordinates responses from other government agencies into a consolidated document.
- This document is then transmitted to a senior official, either a director general or permanent secretary for approval; the minister of foreign affairs (but not usually the president) will sign off on the final document.
- The foreign affairs ministry/department coordinates the delegation to represent the state at the summit.
- Once approved identical sets of documents are then transmitted to those who will be representing government at the summit. Ideally, this is done approximately two weeks before departure to the summit. Where documents are outstanding, this will be indicated in the prepared briefing documents.
- In the case of the president attending the summit, an advance team will visit the location to view premises.

The dissemination of the provisional agenda to member states marks the start of formal preparation for summits. However, preparation begins in practice much earlier – from meetings of legal experts, PRC meetings and ministerial conferences ahead of the summit. In addition, given that there are standard agenda items, preparations can begin on those items also before the agenda is distributed.[84] In Ethiopia, for example, even though at times the Foreign Affairs Ministry receives the agenda only two weeks ahead of summits, preparation begins at least two months in advance.[85]

Normally, the ministries to which the theme for the summit is relevant will be consulted extensively. For example, ahead of the Khartoum summit, which focused on education and culture, the ministries of education in Kenya and Ethiopia were key in formulating the government's position.[86] In Ethiopia, the Africa Affairs Department learnt about it being a theme from the first ministerial conference on this topic that took place in Nairobi. The Ministry of Education and Culture/Tourism provided the Africa Affairs Department with its comments to the report from the ministerial conference.[87] By the time the department received the report of the ministerial conference from the AU Commission, the government position was already prepared. Ahead of the Banjul summit, which had as its theme 'rationalisation of RECs', responsible departments were again consulted. For example, the South African Department of Trade and Industry played a key role in providing information and a position for the government.[88] For the government of Mozambique, which does not have a dedicated ministry on regional integration, a director dealing with integration within the Ministry of Foreign Affairs and Cooperation formed part of the delegation to the Banjul summit.[89] In addition, for the June 2006 Banjul summit, legal officials (for example, the Justice Department of South Africa and the Attorney General's office of Kenya) were instrumental in providing comments to the single legal instrument establishing the merged African Court of Justice and Human and Peoples' Rights and the Charter on Democracy, Elections and Governance.

However, this system does not always work. As of April 2006, the Ministry for the East Africa Community in Kenya had not been informed and asked to comment on the Banjul summit theme of rationalisation of RECs.[90] Women's rights organisations have found that the ministers for gender or women's affairs are not always informed about relevant matters, including texts as important as the Solemn Declaration on Gender Equality in Africa or the Protocol to the African Charter on Human and Peoples' Rights on the Rights of Women in Africa.[91] The much greater range of activities of the African Union compared to the OAU means that the need for consultation and inclusion of other ministries than foreign affairs becomes much more important; yet the mechanisms for this to happen are still faulty in many states.

In some cases, states also use consultants to help prepare for their participation in African Union activities, particularly on extremely technical points. Thus, Algeria called upon a consultant to present the draft protocol on the merger of the African Court on Human and Peoples' Rights and the Court of Justice of the African Union[92] during an African Union experts' meeting held in November 2005 in Algiers.[93]

An example of state preparation processes: Mozambique

The Ministry of Foreign Affairs and Cooperation is responsible for presenting the country's position on AU matters. The minister is assisted by two deputy ministers and the permanent secretary. One of the deputy ministers has responsibility on policy matters over the AU and Multi-lateral Department, which is located in the Africa and Middle East Division.

Once the official in the AU and Multi-lateral Department receives the draft agenda (since 2006 there are three officials in this department), an ad-hoc committee is established. The committee is composed of officials from the following divisions: research and statistics, legal affairs, relations with SADC and finance. Tasks are divided among these officials. Relevant government agencies are consulted: the Ministry of Justice was consulted extensively on the discussions on the single legal instrument establishing a the African Court of Justice and Human Rights. Two documents are prepared: a memo which provides background material; and a position paper, which propose Mozambique's stance on issues on the agenda. Also included is a comment on possible contentious issues at the summit. The documents are transmitted to the deputy minister for review. The foreign affairs and cooperation minister will give a briefing at the president's office. Thereafter, the position is endorsed for the summit. The AU and Multi-lateral Department suggests the composition of the delegation. This is approved by the minister of foreign affairs and cooperation and transmitted to the president for endorsement.

The delegation normally comprises the President, the Minister for Diplomatic Matters located in the President's Office, and the Minister of Foreign Affairs and Cooperation. Officials working on AU matters in the ministry will also form part of the delegation. Additional members from other departments are determined by the theme of the summit.

Engagement with national parliaments

In many of the states considered for this report, the ministry of foreign affairs briefs the parliamentary foreign affairs committee on foreign affairs in general and the progress achieved and problems encountered in relation to the AU. In Kenya, for example, the Minister of Foreign Affairs will include participation at the AU as part of a general activity report to the national parliament.[94] Apart from reporting on AU participation, the minister of foreign affairs will outline priorities and submit a budget for approval by parliament in an annual budget speech. The budget will include the AU contribution and travel costs for AU meetings. The Prime Minister of Mozambique reports to parliament on activities of the cabinet including AU summits.[95]

In the course of our research, we were however unable to find examples of close collaboration between the executive and parliament with a specific view to preparing for the participation of a member state in an African Union summit. This is the case even when states had proposed items for the summit agenda. For example, in 2006 Mali proposed an agenda item for the Khartoum summit relating to youth in Africa based on the conclusions of the *Françafrique* summit held in Bamako in December 2005, and for the Banjul summit on the creation of a research centre on migration, but neither of these proposals were debated in the National Assembly. The government cites the principle of separation of powers to explain this situation, since the constitution forbids parliamentarians to interfere in matters that are within the jurisdiction of the executive.[96]

The South African Department of Foreign Affairs did not formally brief the Foreign Affairs parliamentary sub-committee on the AU specifically, between the Khartoum and Banjul summits.[97] Similarly, a parliamentarian in the Kenyan parliament and representative at the Pan-African Parliament confirmed that reporting to parliament was not done, even in relation to the executive's nomination of a candidate to serve on the African Court on Human and Peoples' Rights.[98]

Composition of national summit delegations

Each state is allowed a delegation of four people who may be accredited to attend the Assembly: the head of state and three others. However, many countries bring far more personnel than the official delegation, even though they will not be able to attend all the relevant meetings.

In the francophone countries, the office of the president of the republic and the relevant departments within the ministry of foreign affairs begin discussions on the size of the delegation that will represent the country to the AU summit, under the supervision of the prime minister, who conducts budgetary arbitration where necessary. Ultimately, the office of the prime minister is responsible for determining the composition of delegations that will represent the country at international meetings.[99] In general, the delegation from francophone countries is composed of persons directly responsible for the items examined both within the ministry of foreign affairs and within the government as a whole, in addition to persons appointed by the office of the president.

The composition of member state delegations in Commonwealth countries will in most instances include the foreign affairs ministry, officials of the AU/Africa directorates within the foreign affairs ministry, the presidency, and the ambassador and staff in Addis Ababa. Officials from the government agency attending to justice matters may also be part of the delegation. At the Khartoum summit where the theme was education and culture, ministers responsible for these issues were also included in some delegations such as that of Kenya.[100] The financial costs for attendance of AU summits and the financial contribution to the AU Commission are borne by the ministry of foreign affairs.

In all cases, the size of a delegation depends on the financial resources of the member state, its interest in the issues to be debated during the summit and above all the possibility of accommodation in the country hosting the summit. For instance, the Banjul summit was attended by Algeria's president, prime minister, minister of foreign affairs and delegate minister in charge of Maghrebian and African affairs; whereas the Malian delegation included only the president and the minister of foreign affairs. Libya, meanwhile, reportedly had a total complement of several hundred people.

There is no real tradition in any of the countries studied of associating civil society with the diplomatic activities of the president or the minister of foreign affairs. However, Mali included women's organisations in the official delegation to the Maputo summit to adopt the Additional Protocol to the African Charter on the Rights of Women.[101] In Senegal, President Abdoulaye Wade has, over the last two years, decided to include two or three students in his official delegation, apparently to introduce them to the management of African affairs.[102]

Upon its arrival at the summit location, the delegation holds a coordination meeting supervised by the ministry of foreign affairs during which the final details of the approach to be adopted during the summit are ironed out to ensure that, with or without the minister, the delegation will uphold the positions of the state. In some cases, the head of state may be consulted if the position prepared has become obsolete due to new developments. There are also often politically difficult agenda items for which decision-making is left to the summit.[103]

5. Regional economic communities and the African Union

The OAU produced two fundamental legal documents that form the basis for Africa's integration: the 1980 Lagos Plan of Action for the Development of Africa and the 1991 Treaty establishing the African Economic Community (also referred to as the Abuja Treaty). The former envisages the development of Africa through regional integration, providing the first legal basis for the creation of regional economic communities (RECs)[104]; the latter proposes the establishment of sub-regional configurations in Africa's five geographical regions and envisages the creation of a continental economic community bolstered by RECs by 2030.[105]

Currently, there are a number of overlapping regional bodies, some of them recognised by the AU and some operating outside AU structures. The following eight configurations are recognised by the AU as RECs: the Economic Community of Central African States, Economic Community of West African States, Common Market for Eastern and Southern Africa, Inter-governmental Authority for Development, Arab Maghreb Union, East African Community, the Community of Sahelo-Saharan States and the Southern African Development Community.[106] Many states belong to more than one of these bodies.[107] There are also competing and conflicting interests between the RECs and the AU: coordination and harmonisation is urgently needed.[108]

One of the objectives of the AU as stated in the Constitutive Act is to 'coordinate and harmonise the policies between the existing and future Regional Economic Communities for the gradual attainment of the objectives of the Union',[109] and the Banjul summit of June/July 2006 was themed on 'rationalisation of RECs'. The Economic Affairs Department of the AU Commission coordinates the relationship between RECs and the AU.

There is no formal legal framework through which RECs engage with the AU. A proposed protocol on relations between RECs and the AU,[110] drafted by the Office of the Legal Counsel and the Economic Affairs Directorate in 2004, would provide such a framework, but the AU has to finalise the draft protocol before it will be open for signatures. The protocol would establish a coordinating committee, including representatives of the heads of the RECs, to monitor the extent that RECs are progressing in the implementation of the Abuja Treaty and ensure the implementation of decisions taken by the Executive Council relevant to RECs.[111]

In the meantime, although RECs accredited to the AU attend summits, where their representatives meet also with the AU Commission, their participation at meetings of the PRC, Executive Council and Assembly of the AU is in practice limited to delivering a single speech (on activities and challenges) and observing proceedings.[112] At the 2006 Banjul summit, for example, the representative of the Southern African Development Community (SADC) made comments only on regional integration and not on other agenda items. On other points it is an individual member state of the REC that will articulate the position of the REC. REC officials believe that the AU should provide a formal opportunity for RECs to state their position on AU summit agenda items.[113]

However, REC representatives do participate in ministerial and other meetings convened ahead of summits under the auspices of the AU. During 2006, specific issues discussed included agriculture, customs policies, infrastructure and trade.[114] There was also a ministerial conference on regional integration in Ouagadougou, Burkina Faso.[115] The meetings closed with resolutions, which were presented to the Executive Council and the Assembly at the summit.

SADC, perhaps the best organised of the RECs in this context, makes regular contributions on legal matters at the AU, including comments to the protocol establishing the AU Court of Justice;[116] while the SADC Secretariat Gender Unit participated in deliberations of the Protocol on the Rights of Women in Africa under the African Charter on Human and Peoples' Rights.[117] The AU focal point at the SADC Secretariat prepares a briefing document for the SADC Council of Ministers meeting in February each year, including issues relevant to the June AU summit; though lack of capacity may prevent adequate responses on some agenda items.[118] The Council meeting will consider and coordinate the positions of member states in relation to the AU agenda.

The SADC heads of state summit in August 2006 discussed the decisions of the July AU summit, and called for a meeting of the troika of the SADC Organ on Defence, Politics, and Security Cooperation to prepare a SADC position on issues relevant to African integration and harmonisation of the RECs prior to the January 2007 AU summit.[119] There was, however, apparently no discussion about the membership in SADC of the Democratic Republic of the Congo, geographically not part of the southern region,[120] nor of the Draft Protocol on the Relations between Regional Economic Communities and the African Union.

The Economic Community of West African States (ECOWAS) is the only REC that has restructured its institutions in order to harmonise them with those of the AU. In January 2006, the Authority of Heads of State and Government, the supreme institution of ECOWAS, decided to transform the ECOWAS Secretariat into an ECOWAS Commission, set up in a similar way to that of the AU. The powers of the ECOWAS parliament were strengthened; the Court of Justice was also restructured in order to separate its administrative and judicial functions; and the Authority also moved further towards the establishment of a new supranational legal regime directly applicable in member states.[121]

Civil society engagement with regional institutions

Efforts by civil society to influence decision-making at REC level have increased in strength as the RECs themselves have acquired a broader agenda and greater importance within the AU. The REC documents in some cases also acknowledge the importance of civil society participation in regional integration. For example, Article 23 of the SADC Treaty reads:

> In pursuance of the objectives of this Treaty, SADC shall seek to involve fully the people of the region and non-governmental organisations in the process of regional integration. SADC shall cooperate with and support the initiatives of the peoples of the region and non-governmental organisations contributing to the objectives of this Treaty in the areas of cooperation, in order to foster closer relations among the communities, associations and people of the region.[122]

The SADC Council of Non-Governmental Organisations (SADC-CNGO), created in 2002 in response to Article 23, is an institution recognised by the SADC Secretariat, though it has still had problems gaining access to the decision-making system of the SADC.[123] The SADC-CNGO held its first civil society forum ahead of the SADC summit in Gaborone in 2005, and the second in Maseru, Lesotho ahead of the August 2006 SADC summit. There the regional representative of ECOSOCC gave an overview of the ECOSOCC structures,[124] and participants also discussed human rights and democracy within the sub-region. NGOs also organise autonomous meetings in the margins of SADC summits. For example, Ditshwanelo, a human rights organisation, held a meeting in the margins of the SADC summit in Gaborone in 2005 to raise awareness of the situation in Zimbabwe.[125]

SADC member states are also supposed to establish 'national committees' of government and civil society,[126] though these are not yet functional in all countries.[127] Botswana, which is also the seat of the SADC secretariat, has a functional national committee, which, according to the Botswana Council of Non-Governmental Organisations, serves as an information-sharing forum on implementation of SADC policies.[128]

More interesting as a model for civil society engagement with an intergovernmental body, however, is the West African Civil Society Forum, established in 2003.

The West African Civil Society Forum

In June 2003, following contacts made by the Nigeria-based Centre for Democracy and Development and International Alert, headquartered in Britain, the ECOWAS Secretariat organised a consultative meeting in Abuja, Nigeria, to analyse issues of regional human security and propose strategies to address them, bringing together participants from civil society organisations, government representatives, donors and experts from the region. The meeting decided to create a number of mechanisms and processes for strengthening human security capacities in the sub-region, including:

- A civil society unit within the Executive Secretariat of ECOWAS;
- An autonomous civil society secretariat to facilitate liaison between West Africa's civil society organisations and ECOWAS institutions;
- A regular Assembly of West African Peoples and Organisations, coinciding with the Ministerial Council meeting preceding the annual summit of the Authority of Heads of State and Government of ECOWAS;
- A joint task force between ECOWAS institutions and civil society to help in developing a strategic plan for safeguarding human security in West Africa and an operational and resource mobilisation plan for implementing such strategy.[129]

In December 2003, the first West African Civil Society Forum (WACSOF) took place in Accra, Ghana, sponsored by ECOWAS and with the participation of over 150 people representing 100 organisations. The forum adopted a charter to govern the new body, and a programme of action for the short, medium and long term.

WACSOF is a membership organisation[130] based on relevant community norms.[131] Importantly, it is not an organ of ECOWAS but a free-standing body funded primarily by external donors.[132] Its objectives include the pursuit and promotion of permanent dialogue and engagement between civil society organisations in the sub-region, ECOWAS and national authorities, and supporting the process of political and socio-economic development and integration of the sub-region and Africa.[133] Two deliberative organs (the Peoples' Forum and the Executive Committee), technical organs (ten working committees elected by the Peoples' Forum for a period of two years [134]) and an executive organ (the secretariat led by a secretary-general) constitute the structure of WACSOF.

The Peoples' Forum is composed of all the representatives of the civil society organisations registered as members of WACSOF and all the associate members; its meetings are also attended by observers, including representatives of the ECOWAS Secretariat.[135] The Peoples' Forum meets annually prior to meetings of the ECOWAS Authority and Council of Ministers.[136] The Forum reviews the activities of the ECOWAS Secretariat and ECOWAS member states and makes appropriate recommendations to the summit, considers the report of the secretary-general as submitted to it by the Executive Committee, approves the appointment of the secretariat upon the recommendation of the Executive Committee, and annually appoints a civil society focal point in each country, which liaises between WACSOF Secretariat, WACSOF members in the country and ECOWAS organs based in the country.

The Executive Committee is elected by the Peoples' Forum, and is responsible for the functioning of WACSOF between sessions of the Peoples' Forum and for appointing the secretary-general and other staff.[137] Members of the Executive Committee are elected for a term of two years renewable once and attend the meetings of the organs and components of ECOWAS.[138]

Soon after its establishment, the ECOWAS Council of Ministers and Authority of Heads of State and Government of ECOWAS expressed support for the creation of WACSOF and called on the ECOWAS Secretariat to support and collaborate with the new body.[139]

WACSOF has so far organised three annual forums, each of which has adopted recommendations for the ECOWAS Council of Ministers to transmit to the heads of state and government.[140] These recommendations have dealt with a variety of subjects, including regional integration, democracy, good governance, human rights, corruption, globalisation, gender issues and trafficking in persons.[141] WACSOF has sent observer missions to elections in West Africa[142] and has held regular meetings with ECOWAS organs, participating in consultations related to programme reviews as well as attending official meetings. WACSOF has established national sections in Burkina Faso, Guinea Bissau, Liberia, Mali, Niger, Nigeria, Sierra Leone and Togo.

WACSOF has not spent much time considering the AU. However, in its first communiqué, it expressed its reservations on the 'process of establishment of norms and standards in relation to governance under the form of an African Peer Review Mechanism (APRM)'.[143] The recommendations from the last forum in Accra, 'invited ECOWAS member states to take concrete steps to implement the Solemn Declaration of the AU on Gender Equality' within the west African region.[144] The Hissène Habré case was considered during the forum held in Niamey, Niger, at the request of Senegalese organisation RADDHO, a member of the WACSOF Executive Council, but no recommendation was adopted by the forum.[145]

Despite the strength of the model in theory, WACSOF has not yet had a significant impact on the functioning of ECOWAS nor has it contributed to a greater awareness among West African citizens about the vision and mission of ECOWAS. This is in part attributable to the newness and inexperience of the network, but also the institutional weakness of the organisations that make up the forum and their lack of knowledge of ECOWAS and the issues relating to African integration.[146]

6. THE AFRICAN UNION COMMISSION: OUTREACH TO CIVIL SOCIETY

Within the AU Commission, the African Citizens' Directorate, located in the Office of the Chairperson of the AU Commission, is the focal point mandated to facilitate civil society contributions to the decision-making processes of the AU, including the summits. Other departments of the AU Commission also independently consult with civil society and seek their views on AU policy: the Women, Gender and Development Directorate, also located in the Office of the Chairperson, has been exemplary in this regard.

Perhaps the most important consultative process of the AU Commission was the development of its 'vision and mission', led by Chairperson Konaré during the period after his appointment in 2002. Since this initial outreach, many civil society organisations have the sense that the enthusiasm of the Commission – and the AU generally – for non-state participation in policy development has waned.[147]

The African Citizens' Directorate

The African Citizens' Directorate, known as CIDO, headed by Dr Jinmi Adisa, is the new name and status for the former unit of the OAU Secretariat supporting the Conference for Security, Stability, Development and Cooperation in Africa (CSSDCA).[148] It is responsible in principle with facilitation of all civil society engagement with the AU organs and processes, including in its constituency both African citizens in Africa and in the diaspora.

The CSSDCA was established by a Solemn Declaration at the OAU summit in Lomé, Togo in 2000, and reinforced by a Memorandum of Understanding adopted at the 2002 Durban summit, outlining commitments on peace and security, human rights, democracy, and governance.[149] The CSSDCA Unit, which was located in the secretariat of the OAU, was responsible for monitoring member state commitments under the CSSDCA memorandum, and also for promoting civil society engagement with the CSSDCA process. As part of its activities, the unit organised the first OAU-civil society conference in June 2001. The meeting examined cooperation between the OAU and civil society and recommended the appointment of a focal point for civil society relations.[150] A second conference took place a year later, also under the auspices of the CSSDCA Unit, and reviewed the proposed statutes to govern ECOSOCC (see below).

With the OAU's adoption in October 2001 of the New Partnership for Africa's Development (NEPAD), the CSSDCA began to be eclipsed in AU debates. Reflecting this change in programming priorities, as well as the new role of ECOSOCC, the CSSDCA Unit was given a new name as the African Citizens' Directorate in late 2005.

CIDO's current responsibilities fall into three areas: liaison with civil society organisations on the continent; outreach to the diaspora outside Africa; and secretariat functions for ECOSOCC. Among CIDO's activities have been ongoing work for the finalisation of the ECOSOCC interim structures; coordinating 'conferences of intellectuals' from Africa and the diaspora in Dakar, Senegal in 2004, and Bahia, Brazil in 2006;[151] developing a plan of action for 'practical, effective and sustainable relations between civil society organisations and the peace, security, democracy and governance agenda of the AU'; and facilitating the implementation of Article 20 of the protocol establishing the Peace and Security Council allowing for civil society participation.[152] As of November 2006, CIDO's staff was to be increased to six people from only two, which should substantially increase its capacity.

CIDO has played an important role in reaching out to civil society organisations, and the existence of the office has meant that the AU Commission is more open to African citizens than the OAU Secretariat was. However – perhaps for reasons of capacity which are now being addressed – it has not advertised information about its activities or availability as a liaison point to assist civil society organisations wishing to contact the AU, either on the website or at civil society meetings other than those organised by the AU itself.

The African Union-Civil Society Organisation Forum

The AU-Civil Society Organisation (CSO) Forum, an event organised by CIDO ahead of the AU summits, is an opportunity to brief civil society organisations on relevant developments within the AU. It is also has the potential to be an opportunity for civil society organisations to inform AU policy by submitting recommendations to the summit. The first AU-CSO forum took place in July 2004 in Addis Ababa, Ethiopia; the second before the Abuja summit in January 2005, and the third in Banjul in July 2006. CIDO has funds to pay for fifty participants at the forum, and in principle self-funded participants are also welcome to attend.

The AU Commission was unable to convene these gatherings ahead of the Sirte (June 2005) and Khartoum (January 2006) summits due to 'logistical and political difficulties'.[153] Civil society actors who attempted to seek the assistance of AU Commission staff to secure visas to attend the summit were met with this helpless response: 'Dear colleagues, the Director has asked me to inform you that unfortunately due to host government guidelines, the AU will not be able to invite any more NGOs and other partners to the summit in Libya. We hope to be able to invite your Group to such meetings in future.'[154] Although there were reportedly genuine problems with providing sufficient accommodation for delegates to the summits in Sirte and Khartoum, it was reasonably clear that the real reason was rather a desire by the host government to exclude civil society organisations from the summit (the AU Commission does not allow host governments to determine who may be invited to such meetings).[155]

There is an attempt at the pre-summit events to have a discussion on the prevailing theme of the AU summit. For example, the June 2006 AU-CSO forum covered the following themes: a progress report on the AU-civil society agenda including a status report on the activities of ECOSOCC; economic integration and the rationalisation of the regional economic communities; and the work of the African Commission on Human and Peoples' Rights.[156] National ECOSOCC chapters were not represented at the meeting, although members of the Interim Standing Committee were present.[157] Proceedings and recommendations from the AU-CSO forum in Banjul were incorporated into a communiqué tabled at the Executive Council of Ministers meeting of 27–29 June.[158] A member of the interim bureau of ECOSOCC, Ayodele Aderinwale, who participated in the AU-CSO meeting, presented the interim ECOSOCC president's report and the resolutions of the forum.

The CSO forums are evidence of the AU's openness to civil society engagement with its processes. However, the quality of the debate is often poor, with a lack of substance, and there are some concerns that the forums are rather used to endorse decisions that have already been taken than to provide a real opportunity for civil society organisations to influence decision-making at the summit – especially since the forums take place some time in advance of the official meetings, making it difficult for participants to stay long enough to engage in direct advocacy with government delegations. In addition, the criteria applied by CIDO in selecting participants to attend forums are not clear; many of those who are invited are quite closely connected to governments, and there have been cases where self-funded participants have been excluded from the meetings, even though they would appear to fulfil the qualifications to attend.[159]

The Women, Gender and Development Directorate and the Women's Forum

The Women, Gender and Development Directorate has convened a two-day women's forum before the AU summits held in July 2004, January 2005 and June 2006. (However, there have been meetings focusing on gender around the time of the OAU/AU summits dating back to the 1998 summit in Ouagadougou, Burkina Faso.) The women's forum brings a number of civil society organisations, particularly but not exclusively from the gender sector, to discuss various items relating to AU policy relevant to gender issues. Ahead of the Banjul summit, the theme for the forum was 'Promoting gender responsive governance in countries emerging from conflict', with the aim of influencing scheduled summit discussions of the AU's strategic position on post-conflict reconstruction and development.[160] The resolutions from the forum – which related to the Protocol to the African Charter on Human and Peoples' Rights on the Rights of Women in Africa, human security, gender parity principles and monitoring and evaluation – were transmitted to the Assembly of Heads of State and Government. For coalitions such Solidarity for African Women's Rights (SOAWR), these events are an opportunity to raise awareness and advocate on a key campaign issue: the speedy ratification and implementation of the Protocol on the Rights of Women in Africa.[161]

Initially, those invited to attend these meetings arranged by the AU Commission, including the pre-summit forum, tended to be the more high-level women's advocates likely to be attending the summit already in their official capacity. Later, a wider range of autonomous women's rights organisations became involved, especially those known to have an interest in working with the AU; the meeting thus tends to be more representative of interested civil society organisations than the general AU-CSO forum. Thus, the women's forum in Banjul demonstrated both a higher quality of debate and a greater sense of strategy in relation to the summit than the main CSO forum. Nevertheless, the criteria for selection and requesting an invitation are still not clear.

The Women, Gender and Development Directorate has led the way in wider consultations with civil society organisations on AU documents and summit preparations, especially in relation to the Solemn Declaration on Gender Equality in Africa and the Protocol on the Rights of Women in Africa. The Gender Directorate has worked closely with SOAWR for several years: it helped to provide space for the coalition to hold a press conference at the Abuja summit in January 2005; hosted a joint meeting with SOAWR in September 2005 to strategise on ratifications and next steps after the Protocol came into force; collaborated with SOAWR in holding a symposium on women's rights and Islam held in Omdurman during the January 2006 Khartoum summit; and jointly produced with SOAWR a document on 'Breathing Life into the African Union Protocol on Women's Rights in Africa', which was launched at the July 2006 Banjul summit.[162] The Women and Gender Directorate has also worked with Femmes Afrique Solidarité and the Africa Leadership Forum to hold consultative meetings in Abuja in January 2005, Libya in July 2005, and in Addis Ababa in May 2006, to put in place strategies for the implementation of the Solemn Declaration on Gender Equality in Africa.[163] The Directorate has also used the African Union website to solicit inputs on its work more widely.[164]

Women's rights organisations lead the way in advocacy at the African Union

Women's organisations have probably been the most successful in engaging the African Union, thanks to coordinated strategies and continent-wide coalitions. Following the 1993 World Conference on Human Rights held in Vienna, with its slogan 'women's rights are human rights', and the 1995 Beijing World Conference on Women, women's rights organisations were galvanised around the world, including in Africa. Their organisation and persistence is reflected in the adoption of the Protocol on the Rights of Women in Africa to the African Charter on Human and Peoples' Rights, by the Maputo summit of the AU in July 2003, followed the next year by the Solemn Declaration on Gender Equality in Africa, at the Addis Ababa summit.

The Protocol on the Rights of Women in Africa arose from a process that began at the African Commission on Human and Peoples' Rights, which has traditionally been very open to civil society contributions. At the African Commission session in Nouakchott, Mauritania, in April 1997, a group of women's rights activists, led by Women in Law and Development in Africa (WILDAF) and the African Centre for Democracy and Human Rights Studies, with the support of the International Commission of Jurists, prepared the first draft of what ultimately became the Protocol. Endorsed by the African Commission, and supported by the Commission's special rapporteur on women's rights, this draft was submitted to what was then the OAU Secretariat, merged with existing texts there, and thus became the foundation of what is one of the most far-reaching documents on women's rights globally.

Meanwhile, the organisation *Femmes Afrique Solidarité* (FAS) led an initiative to form an African Women's Committee for Peace and Development, with a secretariat located at the UN Economic Commission for Africa (now at the Women and Gender Directorate of the AU Commission). FAS, working with this committee and with civil society networks such as the African Women's Development and Communication Network (FEMNET), coordinated action leading to the AU adopting the principle of gender parity in appointments to AU organs and the first ever open debate on gender equality in Africa among heads of state, held at the July 2004 summit in Addis Ababa. The summit adopted the Solemn Declaration on Gender Equality in Africa, committing African leaders to action to address a range of issues affecting gender equality, including the impact of HIV/AIDS on women. FAS has remained active in working with the AU Women and Gender Directorate to devise follow-up strategies to bring the declaration into effect.

Coming together under a coalition named Solidarity for African Women's Rights (SOAWR), Equality Now, FEMNET, the African Centre for Democracy and Human Rights Studies and Akina Mama wa Afrika among others, have also successfully advocated for the speedy ratification and popularisation of the Protocol on the Rights of Women in Africa. SOAWR has produced a range of advocacy materials, including red, yellow and green cards rating African states on their progress towards ratification; engaged the responsible officials of member states at AU summits and at home; worked with the AU Commission and the special rapporteur on women's rights of the African Commission on Human and Peoples Rights; and joined forces with local organisations to hold African States accountable to their commitments to women. As a result of these efforts the Protocol on the rights of Women in Africa came into force in November 2005, setting a record for speed for OAU/AU human rights instruments.

7. THE ECONOMIC, SOCIAL AND CULTURAL COUNCIL

The Economic, Social and Cultural Council (ECOSOCC) is the primary structure directed at facilitating civil society engagement with the AU institutions. However, its role in the decision-making processes of the Union is not yet clear. The organ is still in the process of being established in its final form, and there remains significant lack of clarity on the types of organisation that can be members, how they will be chosen, how its leadership structures will be filled, and what the powers of the body will be beyond simply airing issues of concern to civil society organisations.[165]

Observers of the ECOSOCC process interviewed for this report expressed significant levels of concern at the fact that it is and will remain a body under the control of the AU, rather than an autonomous framework, and that its role is currently purely advisory. However, this integration also provides an opportunity, and there was consensus that the aim of ECOSOCC should ultimately be to provide a genuine voice for civil society in AU discussions. If this is to be achieved, there is a need for the ECOSOCC structures to become more democratic and participatory.

Legal framework

ECOSOCC is an institution established under the Constitutive Act of the AU[166] designed to give civil society organisations a voice within the AU institutions and decision-making processes. It is an advisory organ of the AU consisting of civil society organisations from a wide range of sectors, including labour, business, service providers and policy think tanks.[167] ECOSOCC is viewed as a vehicle through which 'the aspirations of African peoples are met, and operational, institutional and human capacities of African civil society are built and sustained'.[168]

Unlike, for example, the Peace and Security Council, there is no protocol to the AU Constitutive Act establishing ECOSOCC, and the status of the organ is based rather on statutes adopted by the Assembly of the AU. This means, importantly, that ECOSOCC's status can be amended easily, without the need for a lengthy ratification process by member states.

A working group nominated by the interim chairperson of the AU at the time, prepared the draft statutes of ECOSOCC in 2002. This draft was reviewed by an AU-CSO working group created by participants at the civil society forum organised by the CSSDCA unit in June 2002 ahead of the AU summit held in Durban. A revised draft was presented to the 4th Ordinary Session of the Executive Council of Ministers in Maputo in July 2003. Further consultations on the draft statutes took place under the auspices of the AU Commission.[169] The Assembly of Heads of State and Government finally adopted the ECOSOCC Statute in Addis Ababa, in July 2004.[170]

According to its statutes, the objectives of ECOSOCC include the promotion of African civil society participation in the 'implementation of the policies and programmes of the Union', and support of programmes to 'foster rapid political and social and economic development and foster integration in the Continent'.[171]

The criteria for eligibility to participate in ECOSOCC have been controversial, in particular the requirement that 'the basic resources of [an organisation seeking membership] shall substantially, at least 50 per cent, be derived from contributions of the members of the organisation'.[172] Intended in part to exclude 'foreign' or 'international' organisations from ECOSOCC, this rule also effectively excludes a large proportion of, for example, human rights organisations, think tanks and other groups likely to be critical of AU activities.

ECOSOCC's organs are the General Assembly, Standing Committee, Sectoral Clusters Committees and Credentials Committee. For the time being, these only exist in interim form. The 150-member General Assembly is the highest decision-making body. It is responsible for electing members to the Standing Committee, reviewing the activities of ECOSOCC, and approving and amending the rules defining the conduct for CSOs 'affiliated to or working with the Union'.[173]

The CSSDCA Unit convened a meeting in 2003 where participants nominated a 20-member provisional ECOSOCC working group.[174] Approximately 160 representatives of civil society across sectors and including women and youth then met in Addis Ababa in March 2005 as the Interim General Assembly to chart a process for the establishment of permanent structure by March 2007,[175] including the election of an interim bureau (a presiding officer and four deputy presiding officers[176]) and an Interim Standing Committee.[177]

The 15-member Interim Standing Committee, which met for the first time in April 2005, comprises representation from the five regions of Africa – east, south, central, west, north – and special committees.[178] The Interim Standing Committee is supposed to oversee the election of national representatives within the stipulated time, and in June 2005 adopted a two-year strategy to finalise the ECOSOCC structures. As understood by a member of the Interim Standing Committee, their role is to 'take the CSO space made available at continental level to national level', and shepherd the consultative process to elect representatives to the General Assembly.[179] However, ECOSOCC has not yet adopted rules of procedure to govern its operation, although a draft was prepared by the Office of the Legal Counsel in the AU Commission. Office bearers are serving on an interim basis until the permanent structure is endorsed and new elections take place in 2007.[180]

Professor Wangari Maathai, who is a member of parliament and was when appointed a minister in the government of Kenya, serves as the interim president of ECOSOCC until 2007. She is located in Nairobi, Kenya, with a small office receiving financial support from the AU Commission which appears to serves two functions: providing administrative support for the Kenya chapter and performing some secretarial functions of the continental body.

At the AU Commission, the African Citizens' Directorate (CIDO) serves as the secretariat of the ECOSOCC, raising money for the new organ from AU sources, supplying information about AU debates, and providing other support. For example, in a speech at the opening of the AU-CSO forum in June 2006, the head of CIDO informed participants that the interim president of ECOSOCC had 'instructed [him] as head of the [ECOSOCC] Secretariat, to present the conclusions of the report'.[181] CIDO raised US$1 million for the Interim Standing Committee for 2006–07 to assist in the process of finalising the ECOSOCC structures; the Standing Committee believed that more was necessary, but in practice less than half the $1 million had been spent by the end of 2006.[182]

Transparency in the selection process of these representatives is questionable. According to some members of the Interim Standing Committee, they were invited by the AU Commission to attend the March 2005 launch because of their regional and thematic focus.[183] Also, it appears that a number of CSOs invited had a pre-existing relationship with the AU; for instance, the Foundation for Community Development, a Mozambique-based organisation focused on development issues, had a relationship with the Directorate for Women, Gender and Development at the AU Commission.[184] However, many organisations with a profile on issues relevant to the AU were not included, among them sub-regional coalitions which amalgamate national coalitions and thus would appear to be a natural constituency.[185]

Many civil society organisations consulted in the preparation of this report criticised the lack of openness of the election of the interim ECOSOCC structures, the inherent tension in the election of a sitting government representative to be presiding officer of a civil society body, and the reliance on CIDO for support.[186]

ECOSOCC interim national chapters

The Interim Standing Committee at its first meeting in Nairobi in April 2005, agreed that national representatives on the Interim Assembly would initiate national consultations to establish procedures to elect two representatives for each country to serve on the General Assembly to be inaugurated in 2007.[187] The formation of interim national chapters (also referred to as interim national assemblies) was a mechanism to assist in this process. The AU Commission expected the ECOSOCC Interim Standing Committee and its affiliated bodies to raise resources to conduct these consultations if more funds were required than provided by the ECOSOCC interim budget.

Consultations have been held in some regions with a view to strengthening national ECOSOCC chapters and increase the level of participation in ECOSOCC structures. For example, AFRODAD (the African Network on Debt and Development), the representative of southern Africa in the interim bureau, worked with others to convene southern Africa consultations in April and November 2006 as well as national level meetings, with the objective of assisting the definition of a process to elect members to the ECOSOCC General Assembly from the region.[188] Similar consultations have been held in the other regions.

The level of development and indeed knowledge of ECOSOCC varies across the continent, with Kenya the most advanced. In some countries there is no ECOSOCC presence of any kind. In others, ECOSOCC has established a functioning national chapter, but the level of participation and the representativeness of the body is low.

Kenya

In Kenya, the Inter-Region Economic Network, an NGO focusing on social and economic rights, worked closely with the interim president of ECOSOCC in forming an ad-hoc committee to encourage CSO membership onto the national chapter of ECOSOCC and functions as an interim coordinator.[189] The administrative tasks are conducted at the interim president's office. In February 2006, the chapter was launched at a meeting which brought together some one hundred organisations. In October 2006, a national delegates conference elected Kenya's two representatives to serve on the continental body of ECOSOCC.

As of April 2006, approximately 60 NGOs, including development and environmental organisations as well as community-based organisations, had registered with the office of the interim president to be part of the national chapter. Organisations with an Africa-wide mandate and which engage with mechanisms in Africa appear not to be active in the structure – either because, in general, they do not consider the AU as an important forum to engage, or because of the poor dissemination of information on the existence and activities of ECOSOCC.[190]

South Africa

A Department of Foreign Affairs-sponsored and organised conference marked the launch of the South Africa chapter in November 2004. Organisations from several sectors including human rights, faith-based organisations, and the South African National NGO Coalition (SANGOCO) attended the conference, despite some reservations that a government agency was hosting a meeting for a civil society initiative.[191]

The national ECOSOCC chapter is governed by a four-person council.[192] The chair of the Council, who is from the Women's National Coalition, represents the South African chapter on the interim ECOSOCC General Assembly. Another South African representative on the interim body represents the youth. According to the secretary-general of the South Africa chapter, who comes from the African Renaissance Organisation for Southern Africa, these two representatives will also sit on the permanent structure once inaugurated.[193] There is therefore no further process to elect representatives to serve on the General Assembly of ECOSOCC.

The African Institute for Southern Africa offered to host the South Africa chapter temporarily. The secretariat is not staffed adequately to undertake the activities of ECOSOCC full time. According to organisations that participated in the launch or are represented on the body, the South Africa chapter has not met since the November 2004 gathering nor held any preparatory briefing ahead of AU summits.[194] The South Africa chapter of ECOSOCC has met informally with the Department of Foreign Affairs to discuss AU matters, and the government views its relationship with the national ECOSOCC chapter as supportive.[195] The government has, strangely, expressed its reluctance to give a formal briefing to the ECOSOCC chapter ahead of AU summits, as this would 'influence [CSOs] in formulating their position.'[196]

The South Africa chapter of ECOSOCC has experienced difficulties in attracting a strong and diverse group of organisations as members, particularly from the key foreign policy sector, such as the Centre for Policy Studies, the South African Institute of International Affairs, the Electoral Institute of Southern Africa and the Institute for Global Dialogue. These groups have continued to work independently of ECOSOCC. Some of the difficulties relate to the lack of transparency in election of officers to positions within the national structure and to the Interim General Assembly, and the dominance of organisations without any particular focus on AU issues or history of critical commentary on government positions.[197]

Mozambique

The Foundation for Community Development and Liga dos Direitos Humanos represented Mozambique at the launch of ECOSOCC in March 2005. The Foundation for Community Development, which also serves on the Interim Standing Committee of ECOSOCC, has played a coordinating role to raise awareness of ECOSOCC in Mozambique and convened a consultative meeting with local civil society organisations and networks on 20 September 2005.[198] The meeting established a strategic coordinating group of ten organisations representing the ten provinces of Mozambique with the mandate to raise awareness of ECOSOCC in the provinces and to move to elect two representatives to the General Assembly of ECOSOCC.[199] To date, public awareness activities have taken place in three provinces but there has been slow progress, perhaps due to a lack of understanding of the relevance of ECOSOCC by local organisations focusing on issues such as poverty alleviation.[200]

No structures: The Gambia, Ethiopia, Botswana, Senegal, Nigeria

Several countries among those visited for this research had no national level ECOSOCC structures in place. Even though the Gambia has a representative on the Interim Standing Committee – a member of the National Youth Council, a government agency formed to promote the interests of the youth – it does not have a structure to coordinate national activities or arrange elections to the permanent ECOSOCC structures.[201]

The Association of NGOs, an umbrella body of 62 organisations engaged in a spectrum of activities such as education, health and human rights, did not have a relationship with ECOSOCC.[202]

In Botswana neither Ditshwanelo, a human rights organisation which uses African treaty bodies to advance its objectives and collaborates with organisations in southern Africa on human rights issues, nor the 100-member Botswana Council of Non-Governmental Organisations (BOCONGO), were aware of ECOSOCC in that country.[203] In Ethiopia, the government was not aware of the existence of a country chapter of ECOSOCC.[204] Some organisations have had links with AU programmes such as the New Partnership for Africa's Development, yet are not familiar or aware of the existence of ECOSOCC in the country.[205]

Senegal had not established a structure for ECOSOCC, even though several Senegalese civil society organisations have been involved in advocacy relating to the AU, including CONGAD (the *Conseil des Organisations Non-Governmentales d'Appui au Développement*) and RADDHO (the *Rencontre Africaine Pour la Défense des Droits de l'Homme*). There was also no ECOSOCC national chapter in Nigeria. From the official perspective, civil society engagement with AU issues is rather channelled through the national mechanisms related to NEPAD and the APRM.

Evaluation

Arguably, an assessment of ECOSOCC is premature given that it has yet to become a permanent structure. So far, however, a lack of transparent processes and poor communications strategy leads to perceptions of ECOSOCC as a 'club of friends' and that it is packed with government supported organisations with little legitimacy in the wider civil society movement.[206] In particular, there is no clarity on the definition of organisations that should be on the 'electoral roll' of voters nor on the election processes that must be followed to choose the national representatives to the General Assembly.

Yet this should not prevent the institution from engaging with civil society at the national level on its purpose and encouraging broader participation. Collaboration between ECOSOCC and sub-regional CSO collective bodies such as the SADC CNGO and the West African Civil Society Forum could provide a coordinated and structured approach to influencing regional policies effectively.[207] If the issues surrounding the election of representatives to national chapters and the General Assembly are resolved to ensure a more transparent and participatory approach, ECOSOCC has the potential to create new space for civil society engagement with the AU and a new voice for Africa's citizens in the deliberations of the continental institutions.

8. Autonomous civil society engagement with the African Union

Autonomous civil society advocacy – whether by human rights groups, the labour movement, development organisations or other sectors – on AU policies has strengthened over recent years, and must continue to make an important contribution, especially in light of the concerns over the structure and role of ECOSOCC. The AU Commission has been open to such engagement, especially where the civil society organisations or individuals concerned offer particular expertise; however, this openness is variable, and there is also some resistance to autonomous civil society meetings in the margins of summits or statements openly critical of member state or Commission positions.

Effective advocacy with the AU must start well before a summit, with lobbying in national capitals, participation in experts' meetings and other interventions; but participation in summits also provides a critical opportunity for civil society engagement. Perhaps the biggest barrier to such activity is lack of access to information about policies that are up for debate, schedules of meetings and opportunities for participation, and draft texts. Other barriers at the summits include problems in gaining accreditation and obstruction from host governments.

The lack of any Addis Ababa-based organisation with a mandate to facilitate civil society engagement with the AU institutions there means that, if there is any presence at all at critical meetings, it is from only the best-resourced organisations – often African branches of international organisations. The same is true in relation to the NEPAD and APRM secretariats and the Pan-African Parliament, based in Midrand, South Africa. Initiatives to establish organisations to facilitate access by any interested civil society organisation to the AU (but with no agenda of their own) would undoubtedly create a more informed and consistent approach from civil society to AU policy-making.[208]

Access to documents

Perhaps the principal obstacle to effective civil society engagement with the African Union institutions is lack of information. Even though the belated upgrading of the African Union website[209] has improved accessibility of information in recent years, the website remains incomplete (far too many sections bring up the message 'Will be available soon!!!') and has no functioning search capability, so that documents not on the front page are hard to find (though it remains more user-friendly than the NEPAD website[210]). Above all, many documents are simply not posted to the website: these include final documents that have been adopted by the Assembly or Executive Council and are required to be made public by treaty (such as the activity reports of the African Commission on Human and Peoples' Rights); and also draft texts of documents that should be available for public debate by Africa's citizens in advance of their adoption. During 2006, documents in the latter category included the draft text of the Charter on Democracy, Elections and Governance, and the proposals for the creation of a Union government, both of major importance yet both unobtainable without inside contacts in a member state or at the AU Commission. Email requests to the Commission for such documents from unknown requesters typically receive no response.

There is an urgent need for the AU to follow the example of such international organisations as the World Bank and adopt a policy providing for disclosure of documents, except where there is a justified need for confidentiality, and for an adjudication process if disclosure is disputed.[211] In October 2006, the Inter-American Court of Human Rights confirmed the existence of a right of access to information held by government and other public bodies.[212] Even without such a formal policy, draft texts of major new initiatives should routinely be posted to the website and comment requested.

Preparatory meetings

Effective advocacy directed towards a summit depends on patient preparatory work. In those countries where citizens enjoy protection of their right to organise freely, national level contacts and meetings will be the starting point. In several of the countries surveyed for this report, civil society organisations meet informally with officials within the foreign affairs department to influence policy on specific areas of concern, or, especially, to urge ratification of particular treaties. The research for this report found no case of a government actively seeking civil society input, however; and in many cases civil society organisations themselves admitted that they did not engage with government agencies responsible for AU matters before and after AU summits. In Kenya, for example, where there has been active advocacy for the ratification of the Protocol on the Rights of Women under the African Charter on Human and Peoples' Rights, women's rights organisations were not aware of meetings before and after AU summits with the relevant government organisations.[213] An official at the Foreign Affairs Ministry admitted that there was no formal forum between civil society and itself on matters relating to the AU.[214] Since the ambassadors who attend the meetings of the PRC are crucial informants of their government positions, civil society contacts with diplomatic representation in Addis Ababa are also important avenues to influence policy; but again this channel is little used.

At the level of the AU Commission, participation in sectoral experts' meetings at which official texts are drafted can be a very useful route to influence AU policies. For example, the Electoral Institute of Southern Africa (EISA) attended expert meetings during 2006 for the preparation of the Draft Charter on Democracy, Elections and Governance, while women's organisations were heavily involved in the meetings leading up to the adoption of the Protocol to the African Charter on Human and Peoples' Rights on the Rights of Women in Africa. The Directorate on Peace and Security engaged directly with the several organisations, including the Action Support Centre, on establishing an early warning mechanism.[215] Invitations to these meetings is within the gift of the relevant AU Commission department (the Gender Directorate has been particularly open to civil society involvement) and practice varies, while the criteria for selection are not transparent, meaning that participation can be merely tokenistic. It is not unheard of for an organisation to receive an invitation to a meeting without any advance notice or information about what will be discussed.[216]

Observer status and accreditation

Even though preparatory work leading up to summits is critical for long-term success, presence at the summit itself can still play an important role in providing networking opportunities, media visibility, familiarity with processes and personalities, and access to officials and to documentation.

Organisations wishing to engage with member states at summits often encounter difficulties in acquiring accreditation to gain access to public sessions of the summit meetings.[217] To facilitate this process, organisations should apply to the CIDO office in Addis well in advance of a summit, so that the names of the individuals seeking access can be put on the list of those invited by the AU Commission held by the protocol department at the summit venue. However, this system is not advertised anywhere and the numbers who may be granted such assistance are likely to be limited; in practice, individuals must build up their contacts with AU organs in order to obtain such an invitation.[218] If invited by the AU Commission or another organ, civil society representatives can attend the opening and closing sessions of the meetings, and other sessions with the authorisation of the chair, though without the right to speak. Even without accreditation, and depending on the location of the summit, it may be possible to access many common areas used by delegates and engage in direct lobbying.

As a separate process from obtaining accreditation to attend individual summits, criteria for granting observer status with the African Union were adopted by the Executive Council meeting at the Sirte summit in July 2005 – though they are apparently open for review.[219] The criteria provide, controversially, that an organisation wishing to apply for observer status must derive at least two-thirds of its resources from the contributions of its members – thus ruling out virtually all the human rights and policy-focused organisations on the continent.[220] Once granted observer status, the criteria provide that representatives of the organisation may attend public sessions of meetings, be invited to other meetings, have access to non-confidential documentation, etc.

Parallel meetings

The number of meetings organised by civil society organisations in the margins of African summits has been steadily increasing since the creation of the AU. In addition, in January 2006, an ad hoc coalition organised in Nairobi the first independently organised meeting intended to brief interested civil society organisations in advance of a summit, responding to the lack of an AU-CSO forum in Sirte and anticipating problems of access to Khartoum. The meeting adopted resolutions on Sudan's candidacy for the AU presidency and the Hissène Habré case.[221] Especially in countries where civil society does not have a tradition of working on AU issues, the holding of a summit can be an opportunity for national organisations to raise the profile of the continental body and focus on the opportunities it provides[222]: in the case of the June 2006 summit in the Gambia, for example, the Association of NGOs, an umbrella body of NGOs, for the first time convened a meeting on the AU.[223] Several Mozambican civil society organisations, including the Economic Justice Coalition and ABIODES, hosted a meeting ahead of the 2003 AU summit in Maputo, Mozambique, to debate key issues affecting Africa.[224]

A source of frustration for organisations convening such events is formally conveying the resolutions or communiqués to the Assembly of Heads of State and Government or the Executive Council of Ministers; press conferences and other efforts have not always reached the desired audience.[225] Despite its role as a civil society focal point, the African Citizens' Directorate at the AU is not always supportive of the concept of such autonomous meetings that have not sought CIDO's advance authorisation; similarly, the Gender Directorate prefers civil society organisations to come in under the umbrella of the Women's Forum.[226] Civil society organisations themselves need to coordinate better around summit meetings, especially as more groups begin to attend AU events.

Host government obstruction

The major obstacle to civil society engagement at summits in recent years has been obstruction from the host governments. The CSO-AU Forum did not take place in either Libya in July 2005 or Sudan in January 2006, while independent civil society representatives had major difficulties in obtaining visas and had meetings disrupted when they did succeed in reaching the country: in Khartoum, a group of activists meeting to discuss the situation in Darfur were arrested and briefly detained.[227] The Gambia also created difficulties on 'logistical' grounds, preventing a meeting hosted by the international freedom of expression organisation Article 19 and others, which took place in Dakar, Senegal instead.[228]

9. Key decisions at summits in 2006

By way of illustration of some aspects of summit decision-making processes, this section of the report outlines some of the issues arising out of some of the key debates at summits in 2006: the Draft Charter on Democracy, Elections and Governance; the Hissène Habré case; the decision on the chair of the African Union; the decision on the Annual Activity Report of the African Commission on Human and Peoples' Rights; the decision on the Draft Single Legal Instrument on the merger of the African Court on Human and Peoples' Rights and the Court of Justice of the African Union; and the decision on the seat of the African Court on Human and Peoples' Rights.

The Draft Charter on Democracy, Elections and Governance

The Draft Charter on Democracy, Elections and Governance, which was on the agenda of the Executive Council of Ministers meeting at the Banjul summit (and is scheduled to be considered again at the January 2007 summit in Addis Ababa), has its roots in the Declaration on Unconstitutional Changes of Governance in Africa adopted at the Lomé summit of the OAU in 2000.[229] In 2002, heads of state at the Durban summit (the last of the OAU and first of the AU) adopted a further declaration on the principles governing democratic elections.[230] Following this summit, which also saw the adoption of the NEPAD Declaration on Democracy, Political, Economic and Corporate Governance, the AU hosted, with the South African Independent Electoral Commission and the African Association of Electoral Authorities, a continental conference on elections, democracy and governance in April 2003.[231] In 2004, a meeting of government experts discussed these issues, and recommended that the declaration be developed into a new Charter on Democracy, Elections and Governance; the initial draft of this text was debated at an independent experts' meeting held in November 2005. In April 2006, a further experts meeting was held to discuss the draft, immediately followed by a ministerial meeting to provide input from a political rather than technical perspective.[232]

The draft text emerging from these discussions was presented to the AU summit in Banjul, but not adopted. Among the reasons were management of time in the Executive Council meetings, such that there was not a quorum when the text came to be debated, but above all the lack of a real process of political consensus building – among both member states and African citizens – in the period leading up to the summit. The adoption of United Nations documents of similar importance are typically preceded by a series of meetings of several weeks each, attended by both technical experts and government representatives, so that the final draft text debated at a summit will contain only a few 'bracketed' items whose significance is clearly understood. But as in the case of many similar AU texts, the preparatory discussions of the draft charter were of no more than two days each, with documents distributed to participants only a few days before the meetings, making preparation and consultation all but impossible. Meanwhile, although a select few civil society organisations were invited to the meetings of independent experts, there was no attempt to make the draft text more widely available, even by publishing it in full on the AU website. The failure to come to a decision on the Charter in Banjul is thus illustrative of wider problems in the system for drafting and adoption of such texts.[233]

The Hissène Habré case

One of the key decisions considered at both the Khartoum and Banjul summits in 2006 was the position of the African Union in relation to the request of Belgium for extradition from Senegal of the former president of Chad, Hissène Habré, after a Belgian judge delivered, on 19 September 2005, an international warrant to arrest Hissène Habré for crimes against humanity, war crimes, acts of torture and serious violations of international humanitarian law.[234] Senegal's highest court, the Cour de Cassation, had ruled in 2001 that Senegal did not have the jurisdiction to try Habré; and in November 2005 the Indictments Chamber of the Court of Appeal refused jurisdiction to rule on the extradition request.

Senegal decided to refer the case to the January 2006 African Union summit in order for it to indicate 'the competent jurisdiction to try this case'.[235] In the note presenting the case to the African Union, the Senegalese authorities affirmed that 'the case relating to the request to extradite Hissène Habré is closed in Senegal'.[236] However, it appears that Senegal did not circulate documents sufficiently in advance of the summit to allow other delegations to take an informed decision: one west African minister of foreign affairs complained in late December, just weeks before the summit, that he had unsuccessfully sent requests to his Senegalese counterpart asking to be briefed about the particulars of the case.[237]

At Khartoum, heads of state dodged the need for an immediate decision by requesting the chair of the AU Commission to 'set up a committee of eminent African jurists to consider all aspects and implications of the Hissène Habré case as well as the options available for his trial' and report to the July 2006 summit.[238] The committee appointed by Chairperson Konaré met in Addis Ababa in May 2006 and decided to recommend that there should be a preference for an African solution to the matter and that Senegal was the most suitable country to hold the trial although an ad hoc tribunal could also be established.[239] The Assembly accordingly decided to mandate Senegal to prosecute and ensure that Hissène Habré be tried, on behalf of Africa, by a competent Senegalese court with guarantees for fair trial.[240]

This decision by the Assembly is the first intervention by the African Union to implement the principles of the Constitutive Act establishing the Union's 'right ... to intervene in a Member State pursuant to a decision of the Assembly in respect of grave circumstances, namely: war crimes, genocide and crimes against humanity' as well as its 'condemnation and rejection of impunity and political assassination'.[241] However, the decision can be criticised on legal grounds, since there is an ongoing legal proceeding, and Senegal has not officially responded to the Belgian request for the extradition of Hissène Habré, which was based on the relevant provisions of the United Nations Convention Against Torture.

The decision to refer the case to the AU Assembly was an effort by Senegal to escape the political consequences of a legal proceeding in its domestic courts. There was no widespread debate of the case at sub-regional level in advance of the decision to refer, though President Wade of Senegal did meet with President Obasanjo of Nigeria to discuss the case.

The Habré case is interesting from the point of view of civil society engagement with the African Union because of the important role played by a coalition of African (mostly Senegalese and Chadian) and international human rights organisations in bringing the initial complaint against Habré in Senegal. It illustrates both the success and the risks that can arise from confrontational tactics. The prominent role of US-based Human Rights Watch in the case brought resources and media exposure to the victims of President Habré that they would have been unlikely to obtain independently, and was key to the decision of Belgian prosecutors to bring a case against

Habré under the torture convention. The coalition distributed a 15-page document to foreign ministers and diplomatic advisers as well as AU Commission officials in advance of the Khartoum summit summarising the case and presenting different possible options for the AU; a more detailed document was prepared for the Committee of Eminent Jurists and clearly influenced their reasoning. But the international advocacy and especially the Belgian indictment also generated resistance from African states, including Senegal, to non-African involvement in an African legal case, and may have made more difficult the efforts of African human rights groups to advocate for the Senegalese courts to take jurisdiction; and subsequently, when the *Cour de Cassation* (Senegal's highest court) refused to do so, for Senegal to extradite Habré to Belgium.

Decision on the presidency of the African Union

Under the OAU the presidency of the organisation was a largely symbolic role, held by the head of state of the host of the last annual summit. The creation of the African Union and the increased responsibilities now given to the presidency in inter-African relations and conflict resolution has also increased the competition for the post.

In principle, the president of the Union is elected by the Assembly at the January summit (usually held in Addis Ababa), 'after consultations among the member states',[242] for a period of one year. In the event that the Assembly takes place in one of the other member states, the head of state of the host country has the right to chair the session of the Assembly.[243]

It is the Union's practice that the presidency should rotate across the regions of Africa. Thus the presidency of the AU for 2006 was due to be assumed by a member state in the eastern region. Between 2001, when the Constitutive Act entered into force, and 2004, the determination of the acting chairmanship did not pose any real problems. President Thabo Mbeki, whose country, South Africa, organised the first summit of the African Union in Durban, succeeded the president of Zambia, who was the last chairman of the OAU. The following year, President Joachim Chissano, whose country, Mozambique, hosted the second AU summit, took over the leadership of the Union from his South African colleague.

In June 2004, the third ordinary session of the Assembly was held in Addis Ababa, the headquarters of the Union, and President Olusegun Obasanjo of Nigeria was elected chair. During this summit, some voices were raised among the state delegations in attendance as well as within civil society organisations to protest against the decision to host the fifth summit of the Union in Khartoum and the possible accession of Sudan to the chair of the African Union, particularly in light of the massive human rights violations in the Darfur region and the continuing civil war in the southern part of the country. How could the African Union be chaired by a country whose leaders had been investigated and accused of being implicated in violations of humanitarian law by a United Nations commission of inquiry? International opposition to the presidency of Sudan, both from non-governmental organisations and states, was also strong. The summit condemned the human rights violations in the Darfur region and decided to hold the fourth summit of the African Union in Nigeria, pending the resolution of the situation in Darfur.[244] The summit also decided to increase the frequency of the meetings of the Heads of State and Government to two ordinary sessions annually.[245]

The January 2005 fourth summit, held in Abuja, noted some progress in the situation in Sudan, with the signing of a general peace treaty between the government and the Sudan People's Liberation Movement/Army, and decided that the fifth summit, later that year, would be in Sirte, Libya, and the sixth summit would exceptionally be held in Sudan.[246] The summit also extended the mandate of President Obasanjo as president of the AU to January 2006.[247]

The 6th summit took place from 16–24 January 2006 in Khartoum, and its agenda included the election of the president of the Union, presumed (though not required) to be due to come to Sudan. But although eastern Africa supported the Sudanese candidacy,[248] west and southern African states opposed the election of Sudan and its president as chair of the African Union, because of continuing human rights violations in Darfur and the decision of the International Criminal Court to open an investigation into Sudanese officials named in the UN investigation.[249]

The government of Botswana in particular played a key role, taking a principled decision that a Sudanese presidency would be inappropriate.[250] Botswanan president Festus Mogae, 'presumably because of the apparent absence of a vested interest in the Eastern region', chaired intensive discussions to resolve the matter among a committee of seven heads of government.[251] Finally, a compromise was reached by which the Republic of Congo, representing central Africa, assumed the chair.[252]

Civil society organisations again played an important role in keeping the violations in Darfur in the forefront of the considerations of member states. Representatives of the Darfur Consortium (a coalition of several tens of organisations) issued a press release at the summit asserting that 'the Darfur peace process would be jeopardized if African leaders elect a President for the African Union who is a party to the conflict'.[253] A meeting held by the Darfur Consortium in Khartoum to discuss this position was disrupted by the Sudanese authorities and all the participants arrested: the international publicity for this event ended any remaining chance that Sudan might get the presidency.

Annual Activity Report of the African Commission on Human and Peoples' Rights

Article 54 of the African Charter on Human and Peoples' Rights provides that 'the Commission [on Human and Peoples' Rights] shall submit to each ordinary session of the Assembly of Heads of State and Government a report on its activities'. In practice, the session in which the report is reviewed begins with a preliminary presentation of some fifteen minutes by the chairperson of the African Commission on Human and Peoples' Rights, followed by a debate on all the subjects addressed in the report and a decision to adopt it. The report and the decisions on individual communications that it contains only becomes public after this decision. In 2003, the Assembly decided to mandate the Executive Council to assess the work of the Commission.[254] Since that decision, the session of the Executive Council dedicated to the review of the report of the African Commission has become one of the highlights of the African Union summits: while the heads of state and government often adopted the reports without a debate, the ministers of foreign affairs have made a habit of devoting an average of three hours to the report.

The length of debate does not, however, reflect a new interest of member states in ensuring respect for human rights on the continent, but rather a new determination by several states criticised in resolutions by the African Commission to defend their image. Eritrea, Ethiopia, Sudan, Uganda and especially Zimbabwe have complained that the African Commission has adopted resolutions on the human rights situation in their respective countries based on information allegedly obtained from non-governmental organisations without verifying its accuracy with the states in question.[255]

At the Khartoum summit, Sudan accused the Commission of bias because it did not, in the disputed resolution, condemn the rebels of Darfur for the human rights violations that they also allegedly committed; while Uganda pointed out that the text of the resolution did not mention the source of the information of the African Commission and that, as a state party to the African Charter, it had the right to be heard by the African Commission before the adoption of the resolution. Zimbabwe, for its part, was much more virulent towards the continental organ, which it accused of spreading false information conveyed by its enemies, particularly Amnesty International and the British government.

After a debate lasting over three hours, the Executive Council requested the concerned member states to make their views available to the African Commission and the Commission to submit a report at the next summit in Banjul.[256] At its next session, the African Commission heard, in a private session, the representatives from Ethiopia, Uganda and Zimbabwe and considered written comments from these states and from Sudan, which it appended to the 20th activity report submitted to the Banjul summit.[257]

During the review of the 20th Activity Report of the African Commission by the Executive Council at Banjul, Ethiopia, Uganda, Sudan and Zimbabwe complained that the African Commission had not changed its opinion on the human rights situation in their respective countries despite their submissions. In their view, that raised a serious issue regarding the independence of the continental institution.[258] Other states, including Namibia, Swaziland and (more disappointingly) Botswana, supported these assertions. On the strength of this sub-regional solidarity, Zimbabwe accused the Commission of not having respected the decision made by the Assembly by not submitting to the state for comment a decision on an individual communication brought by the Zimbabwe Human Rights NGO Forum.[259]

In her response, the chairperson of the African Commission noted that Zimbabwe had been represented and argued its case before the Commission throughout the hearing of the communication, in accordance with the Commission's rules of procedure and the African Charter.[260] The Commission also asserted that the practice whereby the Union authorises the adoption of its Activity Report is not in conformity with the letter of Article 59 of the Charter, which operates a very clear distinction between decisions on individual communications, which must be approved by the Assembly of the Union, and other decisions which it may take in the context of its mandate and of which it only informs the Assembly.[261]

The Executive Council decided to authorise the publication of the 20th Activity Report of the African Commission and its appendices 'with the exception of that containing Decision 245 concerning Zimbabwe'. At the same time, it invited Zimbabwe to submit its observations on the disputed decision to the African Commission within two months, and the African Commission to submit a report to the Executive Council at its next ordinary session. In addition, the Executive Council requested the states to 'communicate their comments on the Decisions to be submitted to the Executive Council and/or the Assembly within two months of the notification by the African Commission on Human and Peoples' Rights'.[262]

The open challenges to the African Commission's mandate, independence and working methods have brought a response from the Commission, which organised a joint 'brainstorming session' with the AU Commission following the Khartoum summit in January 2006, attended by all of the AU structures concerned by human rights issues. Following the Banjul summit, the Commission decided to revise its Rules of Procedure; prepare a paper for submission to the African Union on its relations with the different AU organs; review the issue of the independence of its own members; and take initiatives towards closer collaboration with NGOs, national human rights institutions and international organisations involved in human rights issues. A special meeting between the African Commission and the AU Permanent Representatives Committee was scheduled for October 2006 with a view to raising the awareness of PRC members of the problems of the human rights body.

Wider publicity about these issues would help the African Commission to refocus the current debate on the responsibilities of the states to promote and protect human rights. Human rights organisations should organise to defend the premier continental institution responsible for defence of human rights.

The Draft Single Legal Instrument on the Merger of the African Court on Human and Peoples' Rights and the Court of Justice of the African Union

The AU Assembly of Heads of State and Government decided to merge the African Court on Human and Peoples' Rights (established by a protocol to the African Charter on Human and Peoples' Rights to complement the African Commission on Human and Peoples' Rights) and the Court of Justice of the AU (provided for in the Constitutive Act) at the June 2004 summit in Addis Ababa, Ethiopia. The AU Commission was instructed to explore the modalities for the merger of the two courts.[263]

Deliberations on the Draft Single Legal Instrument on the Merger of the African Court on Human and Peoples' Rights and the Court of Justice of the African Union began in Algiers in November 2005, where a draft text prepared by the Algerian minister of foreign affairs, a former president of the International Court of Justice, was considered by a working group of PRC. The PRC presented its report on these deliberations to the Khartoum summit in January 2006 and was instructed to hold further deliberations. Civil society initiatives such as the Coalition for an Effective African Court on Human and Peoples' Rights were able to play an influential role in monitoring and engaging with delegations during the preparatory stages ahead of the summit, including by proposing a draft text for the merger protocol.

The AU Commission, under the auspices of the Office of Legal Counsel, convened on 16–19 May 2006 a meeting of ambassadors and representatives from the capitals. Some government delegations, notably Kenya and Uganda, included experts outside of government agencies to participate in deliberations on the merger document at the meeting from. During the meeting, Algeria, South Africa, Nigeria, Kenya and Egypt were active in articulating their views on the document. Algeria was keen to see the passage of draft by consensus. Nigeria, one of the backers of the establishment of an integrated court, was also favourable to agreement of the draft by consensus.

However, failure to reach consensus on geographical representation in the composition of the court and on a right of direct access to the court by individuals, meant that the document was referred to the AU summit in Banjul for resolution. The fact that many state delegates had also participated in the preparatory meetings in Algiers and Addis Ababa facilitated the debate at the summit, despite the usual lack of timely documentation. However, eventually, the Banjul summit mandated the AU Commission to convene a ministerial meeting to consider the draft protocol and present recommendations in January 2007 in Addis Ababa.[264] As of November 2006, the AU Commission legal directorate was facing difficulties in scheduling a preparatory meeting in advance of the summit, because of the pressure of competing meetings.

The seat of the African Court on Human and Peoples' Rights

The Assembly decided in January 2005 that the headquarters of the Court of Justice would be in the eastern region.[265] This decision was maintained for the merged court. Mauritius had offered to host the Court of Justice and remained the main contender for the merged court. Towards the end of 2005, Kenya and Tanzania also indicated that they were willing to host the court, but by the time of the January 2006 summit, only Mauritius and Tanzania were still contenders. Without an undisputed host country emerging, the AU requested members of the eastern region to decide which of these countries would host the court. During the Khartoum summit, the delegates of the eastern region met and the matter was put to a vote: Tanzania won the majority of the votes by a narrow margin. Ethiopia, which chaired the meeting as current dean of the region, submitted its report to the AU Commission in which it recorded its discussions and recommended that Tanzania should become the seat of the new court.

However, Tanzania had not yet deposited its instrument of ratification of the protocol establishing the African Court on Human and Peoples' Rights; only states that have ratified the protocols establishing both courts are eligible to host the merged court. Thus, no decision was taken in Khartoum. Since those discussions, Tanzania ratified the protocol establishing the Court in February 2006. The AU finally confirmed Tanzania as the host of the Court at the swearing-in ceremony for the judges on 2 July 2006 at the Banjul summit.[266]

10. UPDATE: JANUARY–NOVEMBER 2007

Introduction

The main focus of the African Union (AU) in 2007 related to institutional reform and the creation of the Union Government. There was much activity in expediting the elections process for the General Assembly of ECOSOCC and making the African Court on Human and Peoples' Rights functional. This section provides new information on these issues since the publication of the report in January 2007, up to early November 2007.

The creation of the Union Government

At the Addis summit in January 2007, the Assembly of Heads of State and Government decided that there would be one central theme and agenda item at the Accra summit in July, a 'Grand debate on the Union Government'.[267] This decision was based on a report prepared by a committee of seven heads of state on African political and economic integration[268] and presented to the July 2006 Banjul summit.[269]

Although the decision called on member states to carry out consultations at national level, in a majority of countries this did not happen. In several countries where there were public meetings to discuss the proposals, including Ethiopia, Ghana, Kenya, Nigeria, Senegal and South Africa,[270] civil society organisations took the initiative to organise these meetings and government officials were invited to participate. In some other countries, ministers did brief parliament, but there was no wider consultation.

In some sub-regions, notably the SADC, governments met to develop a common position on the Union Government.[271] The decision taken by heads of government stated that there should be an assessment of the AU Commission and the RECs and the extent to which the 1991 Abuja Treaty on the Establishment of an African Economic Community has been implemented. The decision further stated that a timetable should be set to achieve the Union Government. In addition, the decision insisted on the need for adherence to the principle of 'subsidiarity', i.e. that member states of the AU are independent, sovereign states belonging to RECs. Civil society did not participate at this session, and there were no formal consultations with civil society groups.

Ahead of the Accra summit, members of the Permanent Representative Committee and Executive Council met in May for a retreat, culminating in an extraordinary session of the ministers of foreign affairs, in Durban, South Africa, where the Union Government and strengthening the AU Commission were discussed.[272] Consensus was not reached by state delegations on the Union Government.

The Assembly of Heads of State and Government discussed the Union Government at the Accra summit from 1–3 July. There were two prevailing views. A group largely led by Senegal and Libya were of the view that the

AU was ready to advance to the Union Government, and, as proposed in the report presented to the Banjul summit, should immediately strengthen the Commission with limited executive powers, expand the Executive Council of Ministers to include sectoral line ministers, and create national commissions for AU Affairs. Other states, led by Botswana and Uganda, proposed that an audit of the AU should be conducted first and an assessment should be made on readiness to advance to the Union Government. In particular, concerns were raised over the challenges facing the AU Commission – the implementing agent of the AU – in achieving this goal. The fact that some of the AU institutions provided for in the Constitutive Act were not in place, including the specialised technical committees and the financial institutions, required investigation.

On the margins of the Accra summit debates were parallel civil society discussions on the Union Government, notably the Roundtable on the Union Government, during the AU/CSO Forum organised by CIDO (20 June); the Continental Civil Society Conference on the African Union Government (22–23 June); the meeting of the Solidarity for African Women's Rights on the Protocol to the African Charter on the Rights of Women in Africa and the Union Government debate (26 June); and the week-long Pan African Youth Leadership Forum organised by Friends of Africa International (18–25 June). Other meetings included workshops with west African media and youth on Economic Partnerships Agreements; and three solidarity events with the peoples of Zimbabwe, Darfur-Sudan and Ethiopia.

Following a heated debate, the Assembly agreed in the form of a declaration to review the state of affairs of the AU with a view to determining its readiness towards a Union Government. In particular, the Assembly agreed (in summary) to:
- Accelerate the economic and political integration of the African continent, including the formation of a Union Government of Africa where the ultimate objective of the African Union is to create a United States of Africa;
- Conduct an audit of the institutions and organs of the AU;
- Review the relationship between the AU and the RECs;
- Find ways to strengthen the AU and elaborate a timeframe to establish a Union Government.[273]

The declaration lastly notes the 'importance of involving the African peoples, including Africans in the Diaspora, in the processes leading to the formation of the Union Government.'

Following this decision, a panel of eminent persons[274] was set up to conduct the 'audit review'. The review team began its work on 1 September. In the second week of October, civil society was invited to submit comments to the panel by 26 October, with an opportunity to make presentations before it on 24 October. Fahamu/AU Monitor, RADDHO, Equality Now/Solidarity for African Women's Rights and AFROFLAG-Ethiopia presented a submission on behalf of 20 organisations. The final text of the review was, according to the terms of reference, to be presented to the Assembly of Heads of State and Government at the January 2008 summit in Addis Ababa.

The terms of reference of the audit review panel include the following:
- Review the current state of affairs, with an in-depth analysis of the dynamics underlining the current situation and provide a factual description and assessment of the state of the Union, particularly as it relates to Africa's quest for economic and political integration taking into account the core values outlined in the Constitutive Act of the African Union;
- Review existing Union decisions and agreements with a view to identifying the challenges and constraints facing Member States with respect to the implementation of agreed decisions and agreements;
- Make an assessment of the degree and conditions of the involvement of civil society and the African population in the process of continental economic and political integration.[275]

Conducting a review of the African Union, its various organs and the regional economic communities, in four months is a rushed process, which limits the possibility for consultation on the proposals. Civil society received only ten days notice to make their submissions. The panel's call for citizens and civil society submissions was posted on the AU website and subsequently distributed via the AU Monitor website and email list (a civil society initiative), ten days before the due date.

The election of commissioners

The four-year terms of the eight commissioners and the chair and deputy chair of the AU Commission came to an end in August 2006. However, the Executive Council decided at the Banjul summit that the method of election of the commissioners be reviewed and the elections be moved to July.[276]

The events leading up to Accra summit and debates over the Union Government and role of the AU Commission postponed the election of commissioners yet again. The retreat for foreign ministers and extraordinary session of the Executive Council of the AU in South Africa from 8–10 May decided to postpone the election of commissioners to 2008.[277] At the Accra summit, the Assembly of Heads of State and Government confirmed that the election of the chairperson and deputy chairperson of the AU Commission would take place in January 2008.[278] The closing date for submission of nominations was changed to 30 October.

Despite the clear framework established in the statutes of the African Union Commission adopted at the Durban summit of the AU in 2002,[279] there have been divisions among member states on the role of the AU Commission in the work of the AU both currently and in future. In some quarters, it is argued that the AU Commission should be a simple implementing agent for decisions of the Assembly and Executive Council. Others believe that in addition to implementation, there should be space to develop policies that will advance integration. As such, the role of the person charged with leading the institution becomes important. Some advocate for a high-profile leader at the level of a former president who will be able to engage with leaders in order to move an ambitious AU agenda forward. Others believe that the AU requires a technocrat who will focus more on implementation of policy. Furthermore, member states are yet to reach consensus on the region the next chairperson of the AU Commission should come from. A further contentious issue is whether the chairperson of the AU Commission should appoint the commissioners – a departure from the current practice where all commissioners are individually elected by the member states.

Developments on the Economic, Social and Cultural Council (ECOSOCC)

Following a meeting of the Interim Standing Committee of ECOSOCC in Cairo in February 2007, processes to expedite the elections process of the ECOSOCC General Assembly began. Included in the mandate of the Standing Committee was the need to raise awareness on the elections process and to ensure the elections took place between June and December 2007.[280]

A Credentials Committee, established under the ECOSOCC Statutes and comprising civil society representatives from Africa's regions,[281] was responsible for reviewing the list of nominations for membership of the General Assembly to ensure it complied with the criteria set out in the ECOSOCC Statutes. The Interim Standing Committee was to consider appeals arising from the nominations and elections process. Qualified CSOs could submit nominations to participate as candidates for election to the General Assembly or to serve on the Electoral College which would oversee the elections.

The Credentials Committee met in Accra from 17–20 June to review the list of nominations submitted and also report to the AU/CSO pre-summit forum from 19–21 June on progress made in finalising the nominations list.[282] The chairperson of the Credentials Committee reported that of the applications received, the pool did not represent all member states. No nominations were received from 33 countries, and as a result the deadline was extended to 15 August.[283]

Ultimately, 218 applications were received from 35 states.[284] No nominations were received from 18 states. From these nominations, as decided by the Interim Standing Committee, the Electoral College consisted of those civil society organisations that did not qualify under the Statutes of ECOSOCC.[285] The elections were scheduled to take place at continental, regional and national level from September to December 2007. The Electoral College and a competent national authority, which the Interim Standing Committee identified as national bodies that register CSOs with the support of the foreign ministry, managed the elections. The monitoring of the elections was done by a designated member of the Interim Standing Committee, a representative of the AU Commission or ECOSOCC secretariat, and a member of the Interim General Assembly. This structure was to be replicated at regional and continental level. The continental elections took place in Addis Ababa on 31 October and eight organisations were chosen as ECOSOCC members.[286]

The elections process has been heavily criticised for lack of transparency by members of the Interim Standing Committee themselves: in particular, it is charged that the process of choosing the Credentials Committee was not clear and in itself problematic; that insufficient efforts were made to popularise the process at national level; and that CIDO exercised too much control over the process, acting as gate-keeper rather than facilitator.[287] It is also clear that the eligibility criteria for ECOSOCC, particularly the requirement that CSOs should have at least 50 per cent of their budgets drawn from within Africa, locks out over 80 per cent of the NGOs that have been working on the African Union.[288] It was significant that many organisations within the Interim General Assembly were considered ineligible from standing for leadership positions at the continental level. In many countries there was no publicity about the elections and it was not clear if in fact elections had taken place as planned, even to organisations that had been involved in ECOSOCC discussions from the beginning. These criticisms reflect widespread concern from the outset at the role played by CIDO in acting as a secretariat for ECOSOCC as well as a focal point for civil society within the AU Commission.

Civil society participation at the Accra summit

The accreditation process for civil society organisations at the Accra summit in July 2007 was once again not clear. Only five CSOs were accredited through the Commission. A larger number of civil society representatives gained access to the summit following protracted shuttling between the Ghana foreign ministry and Commission's Protocol Division and the offices responsible for issuing cards to ascertain whether they had received accreditation. By contrast, media professionals appeared to have a less cumbersome experience. As a result some members of civil society were unable to attend the open sessions of the summit.

INDIVIDUALS CONSULTED FOR THIS REPORT

Jinmi Adisa, Director, African Citizens Directorate, AU Commission, Addis Ababa

Ben Agutu, acting head, AU and Africa Directorate, Ministry of Foreign Affairs, Nairobi

Abiola Akiyode-Afolabi, Women Advocates Research & Documentation Centre (WARDC), Lagos

Minelik Alemu, Counsellor, Legal Affairs General Directorate, Ministry of Foreign Affairs, Ethiopia

Desire Assogbavi, Oxfam GB, Addis Ababa

Gillian Ayong, Action Support Centre, Johannesburg

Maurice Badila, Legal Officer, Ministry of Foreign Affairs, Republic of Congo, Brazzaville

Abdalla Bujra, director, Development Policy Management Forum, Addis Ababa

Savio Carvalho, Oxfam Uganda, Kampala

Faizal Faquir Cassam, Deputy Director, Africa and Middle East Division, Ministry of Foreign Affairs and Co-operation, Mozambique

Jaime Valente Chissano, AU and Multi-lateral Department, Ministry of Foreign Affairs and Co-operation, Mozambique

Rudo Chitiga, consultant, London

Sofiane Chouiter, lawyer, Constantine, Algeria

Peter da Costa, consultant, London

Falifou Diallo, Minister and Special Adviser to the Senegalese president on African issues, Dakar

Maty Diaw, FEMNET, Nairobi

Bineta Diop, Femmes Afrique Solidarité, Geneva

Moussa Diop, Femmes Afrique Solidarité, Dakar

Abie Ditlhake, SADC Council of NGOs, Gaborone

Omar Gassama, National Youth Council, Banjul

Irungu Houghton, Oxfam GB, Nairobi

Couaovi Johnson, Secretary to the AU, Office of the Chairperson of the AU Commission, Addis Ababa

Moses Kachima, Southern African Trade Union Co-ordination Council, Gaborone

Pascal Kambale, AfriMAP, Washington DC

Ibrahima Kane, Interights, London

Amadou Kebe, Ambassador of Senegal to Ethiopia and to the AU, Addis Ababa

Ben Kioko, Director, Directorate of Legal Affairs, AU Commission, Addis Ababa

Stephen Kokerai, Legal Affairs Unit, SADC Secretariat, Gaborone

Souleymane Kone, Technical Adviser, African Union and Regional Cooperation, Ministry of Foreign Affairs, Mali

Kafui A. Kuwonu, WILDAF West Africa, Lomé

Chris Landsberg, Director, Centre for Policy Studies, Johannesburg

Manyepedza P. Lesefedi, Director, Department of Asian and African Affairs, Botswana

Moke Loamba, Association pour les droits de l'homme et l'univers carceral (ADHUC), Brazzaville

Alice Mabote, Liga dos Direitos Humanos, Maputo

Soyata Maiga, Association des Juristes Maliennes (AJM), Bamako

Helder Malauene, Foundation for Community Development, Maputo

Bronwen Manby, AfriMAP, London

Tshepo Mashiane, African Renaissance Organisation for Southern Africa, Johannesburg

Magdaline Mathiba-Madibela, Gender Unit, SADC Secretariat, Gaborone

Khabele Matlosa, Electoral Institute of Southern Africa, Johannesburg

Russel Mezeme M'ba, Counsellor, Embassy of Gabon, Addis Ababa

Babacar Carlos Mbaye, Diplomatic Adviser to the President of Senegal, currently Ambassador of Senegal to Turkey

Nobuntu Mbelle, consultant, Johannesburg

Aboubacry Mbodj, RADDHO, Dakar

Vitalis Meja, AFRODAD, Harare

Zanele Mkhwanazi, South African NGO Coalition (SANGOCO), Johannesburg

Modise Modise, Permanent Secretary for Development, Office of the President, Botswana

Alice Mogwe, Ditshwanelo, Gaborone

Faiza Mohamed, Equality Now, Nairobi

Angelo Mondlane, Policy and Strategic Planning Unit, SADC Secretariat, Gaborone

Moostaq Moorad, Deputy Permanent Secretary, Ministry of Foreign Affairs, Botswana

Allehone Mulugeta, Legal Affairs General Directorate, Ministry of Foreign Affairs, Ethiopia

Roselynn Musa, FEMNET, Nairobi

Mohammed Naimi, Head of Policy Analysis and Research Division, Strategic Planning, Policy Monitoring and Evaluation Directorate, AU Commission, Addis Ababa

Barack Ndegwa, Director, East Africa Community Ministry, Kenya

Dismas Nkunda, International Refugee Rights Initiative, Kampala

Michael O'Brien, African Child Policy Forum, Addis Ababa

Chidi Odinkalu, Africa Legal Officer, Open Society Justice Initiative, Abuja

Eve Odete, Pan Africa Policy Officer, Oxfam GB, Nairobi

Ben Ogutu, Acting Head, AU and Africa Directorate, Kenya

Gabrielle Olea, Counsellor, Embassy of the Republic of Congo, Addis Ababa

Wycliffe Oparanya, Member of Parliament and Pan-African Parliament, Kenya

Steve Ouma, Kenya Human Rights Commission, Nairobi

El Hamdi Salah, Counsellor, Embassy of Algeria, Addis Ababa

Helen Seifu, Ethiopia Women Lawyers Association, Addis Ababa

Rotimi Sankore, CREDO, London

Nthuthang Seleka, Africa Multi-Lateral, Department of Foreign Affairs, South Africa

James Shikwati, Inter-Region Economic Network, Nairobi

Tamre Teka, PANOS Ethiopia, Addis Ababa

Yetunde Teriba, Acting Director, Women, Gender and Development Directorate, AU Commission, Addis Ababa

Alioune Tine, RADDHO, Dakar

Babolokile Tlale, Botswana Council of Non-Governmental Organisations, Gaborone

Ozias Tungwarara, AfriMAP, Johannesburg

Muthoni Wanyeki, Consultant, Nairobi

Ousmane Yabo, Association of NGOs, Banjul

Darwit Yirga and Daniel Yilma, Africa Affairs, General Directorate, Ministry of Foreign Affairs, Ethiopia

Fatimata Dicko Zouboye, AJM, Bamako

Christophe Zoungrana, Africa coordinator, Global Call to Action Against Poverty, Dakar

ORGANISATIONS INVOLVED

AfriMAP

AfriMAP is a project of the Open Society Institute's network of African foundations. The Open Society Institute, a private operating and grant-making foundation, aims to shape public policy to promote democratic governance, human rights, and economic, legal, and social reform. OSI was created in 1993 by investor and philanthropist George Soros to support his foundations in Central and Eastern Europe and the former Soviet Union, and the emerging network in Africa. The Soros foundations network today encompasses more than 60 countries, and includes the Open Society Foundation for South Africa, the Open Society Initiative for East Africa, the Open Society Initiative for Southern Africa, and the Open Society Initiative for West Africa.

AFRODAD

AFRODAD, the African Forum and Network on Debt and Development, is a civil society organisation born of a desire to secure lasting solutions to Africa's mounting debt problem which has impacted negatively on the continent's development process. It mobilises African civil society to engage in advocacy on issues of debt and development with their governments and with creditor governments and institutions. A board representing sub-regions across the continent governs a secretariat based in Harare, Zimbabwe. AFRODAD has affiliates or debt coalition partners in 15 African countries.

Oxfam GB

Oxfam GB works with others to overcome poverty and suffering in 24 countries across Africa. Alongside its development and humanitarian work, Oxfam GB supports regional African organisations and coalitions to effectively engage continental and international policy-making institutions to respond to poverty and exclusion. Recognising the next three years as a defining moment for the African Union, Oxfam GB has invested in partners and its own staff to support the African Union as a positive force for realising the social, economic, political and cultural rights of Africans.

ENDNOTES

a   See final pages of this report and http://www.oxfam.org.uk, http://www.afrodad.org and http://www.afrimap.org/ for more information about the three organisations.

b   'Summit' in this report means the whole series of inter-governmental meetings that take place in one location at one period, including those of the Assembly of Heads of State and Government, the Executive Council and the Permanent Representatives Committee.

c   Algeria, Botswana, Republic of Congo, Ethiopia, Gambia, Kenya, Mali, Mozambique, Nigeria, Senegal and South Africa.

1   The Constitutive Act of the African Union was adopted in Lomé, Togo, in July 2000, and came into force on 26 May 2001. The first AU summit took place in Durban, South Africa in July 2002.

2   Article 2 of the OAU Charter.

3   *Strategic Framework of the African Union Commission, 2004–2007, (FINAL DRAFT)*, 4 March 2004, p.4.

4   *Vision of the African Union and Missions of the African Union Commission, Final Draft*, March 2004, p.18.

5   AU Constitutive Act, preamble.

6   Ibid., Article 3(f).

7   Ibid., Article 4.

8   Ibid., Article 4(h).

9   Ibid., Article 23.

10   Ibid., Article 30.

11   Ibid., Article 3(g).

12   The departments are: the Office of the Chairperson (headed by Chair Alpha Oumar Konaré); Office of the Deputy Chairperson (Patrick Mazimhaka); Peace and Security (Commissioner Said Djinnit); Political Affairs (Julia Dolly Joiner); Infrastructure and Energy (Bernard Zoba); Social Affairs (Bience P Gawanas); Human Resources, Science and Technology (Nagia Mohammed Assayed); Trade and Industry (Elisabeth Tankeu); Rural Economy and Agriculture (Rosebud Kurwijila); and Economic Affairs (Maxwell Mkwezalamba). In addition, headed by directors rather than commissioners, and located in the Office of the Chairperson, are the Office of the Legal Counsel (Adv. Ben Kioko), the Women, Gender and Development Directorate (Acting Director Yetunde Teriba, as of November 2006); the African Citizens' Directorate (Jinmi Adisa); and the Directorates for Conferences and Events (Assoul Boubekei); Programming, Budgeting, Finance and Accounting; and Administration and Human Resources Development.

13   A protocol is under debate to merge the Court of Justice with the African Court of Human and Peoples' Rights; see section discussing key decisions at 2006 summits below. The African Commission on Human and Peoples' Rights is not mentioned as an organ of the African Union in the Constitutive Act, but its authority rests independently on the African Charter on Human and Peoples' Rights; to which there is also a protocol establishing an African Court on Human and Peoples' Rights. The financial institutions include an African Central Bank, African Monetary Fund, and African Investment Bank (Constitutive Act, Article 19), The proposed committees are to be composed of relevant ministers, and are to be dedicated to: Rural Economy and Agricultural Matters; Monetary and Financial Affairs; Trade, Customs and Immigration Matters; Industry, Science and Technology, Energy, Natural Resources and Environment; Transport, Communications and Tourism; Health, Labour and Social Affairs; and Education, Culture and Human Resources (Constitutive Act, Article 14).

14   Protocol Relating to the Establishment of the Peace and Security Council of the African Union.

15   See Article 16, Paragraph 1 of the Rules of Procedure of the Executive Council.

16   See Article 11 of the Rules of Procedure of the Permanent Representatives Committee.

17   Articles 90 and 91of the Treaty Establishing the African Economic Community.

18   African Charter for Popular Participation in Development and Transformation, Arusha, 1990.

19   Constitutive Act, preamble.

20   *Strategic Framework of the African Union Commission*, p.19.

21   *Vision of the African Union and Missions of the African Union Commission, Final Draft*, March 2004, p.31. See also the Kigali Declaration of the 1st African Union Ministerial Conference on Human Rights in Africa, 8 May 2003.

22   *Strategic Plan of the Commission of the African Union, Volume 2: 2004–2007 Strategic Framework of the Commission of the African Union*, May 2004, p.48.

23   The Commission had requested a staff of 1 300 in 2005 and the complement approved by the Assembly was 750, but the budget

approved for 2005 did not allow for employment of the full complement. Interview with official, Office of the Chairperson of the AU Commission, Addis Ababa, Ethiopia, 19 May 2006. The European Commission has a staff of 25 000; see http://europa.eu/institutions/inst/comm/index_en.htm.

24   Structure of Budget and Modalities of Funding, Executive Council, Ninth Ordinary session 25–29 June 2006, Banjul, the Gambia, EX.CL/246(IX).

25   Other states contribute much less: for example, Ethiopia and Botswana contribute 0.63 and 0.83 per cent of the total budget respectively. See Statement of Contributions of Member States to the African Union Budget as at 12 June 2006, Executive Council, Ninth Ordinary Session 25–29 June 2006, Banjul, the Gambia, EX.CL/249(IX) and Decision on the Scale of Assessment, Assembly/AU/Dec.88(V), Sirte, Libya, 2004.

26   See European Commission-African Union Joint Declaration, 2 October 2006, Addis Ababa, available at http://www.europa-eu-un.org/articles/en/article_6309_en.htm.

27   See, *Study on an African Union Government: Towards a United States of Africa*, African Union, undated (2006).

28   The January 2006 summit was an exception, being held in Khartoum, Sudan, due to controversy in 2005 over Sudan's candidacy to be AU president.

29   Decision on the Framework for the Organisation of Future Summits, Assembly/AU/Dec.63(IV). At the inauguration of the AU in 2002, the body held its summits once a year.

30   Interview with official, Office of the President, Gaborone, Botswana, 26 September 2006.

31   Interview with official, Africa Multi-lateral, Department of Foreign Affairs, Pretoria, South Africa, 7 June 2006.

32   Interviews with officials and inputs at consultative meeting, Addis Ababa, 10–11 November 2006.

33   The Rules of Procedure of the Executive Council, Assembly of the African Union, First Ordinary session, 9–10 July 2002, Durban, South Africa, Assembly/AU/2(I); Rules of Procedure of the Assembly of the Union, Assembly of the African Union, First Ordinary Session, 9–10 July 2002, Durban, South Africa, Assembly/AU/2(I)

34   Statutes of the Commission of the African Union, Assembly of the African Union, First Ordinary Session, Assembly of the African Union, 9–10 July 2002, Durban, South Africa, Assembly/AU/2(I).

35   Statutes of the Commission of the AU, Assembly/AU/2(I), Article 8(1)(l) reads that the Chairperson shall, 'circulate the provisional agenda of sessions of the Assembly, the Executive Council and the PRC to Member States,' Article 3 reads that the Commission shall 'organise and manage the meetings of the Union.'

36   Article 8, Paragraph 2 of the Rules of Procedure of the Assembly of the African Union Assembly/AU/2(I)a, p.5.

37   Article 9, Paragraph 2 of the Rules of Procedure of the Executive Council of the African Union Assembly/AU/2(I)b, p.5.

38   See Article 9, Paragraph 2 of the Rules of Procedure of the Executive Council and Article 8, Paragraph 2 of the Rules of Procedure of the Assembly of the African Union.

39   See Article 9 of the Rules of Procedure of the AU Assembly and Article 10 of the Rules of Procedure of the AU Executive Council.

40   See for example Annotated Agenda, Executive Council, Ninth Ordinary Session, 25–29 June 2006, Banjul, the Gambia, EX.CL/Annotated/Agenda(IX).

41   Input at consultative meeting, Addis Ababa, 10–11 November 2006.

42   See Article 9, Paragraph 2(g) of the Rules of Procedure of the AU Executive Council and Article 8, Paragraph 2(d) of the Rules of Procedure of the AU Assembly.

43   Interview with official, Office of the Chairperson of the AU Commission, Addis Ababa, Ethiopia, 19 May 2006.

44   See Article 9 of the Rules of Procedure of the Assembly of the African Union and Article 10 of the Rules of Procedure of the Executive Council.

45   Assembly/AU/8(VI) Add.13

46   Assembly/AU/9(VII) Add.3

47   Assembly/AU/8(VI) Add.12

48   Assembly/AU/9(VII) Add.2

49   Assembly/AU/8(VI) Add.12.

50   See EX.CL/242(VIII) Add.9.

51   See Article 8, Paragraph 3 of the Rules of Procedure of the Assembly of the African Union and Article 9, Paragraph 3 of the Rules of Procedure of the Executive Council.

52   See Article 8, Paragraph 1(m) of the Statutes of the Commission of the African Union.

53   Rules of Procedure of the Executive Council, Assembly of the African Union, First Ordinary Session, 9–10 July 2002, Durban, South Africa, Assembly/AU/2(I).

54   Interview with official, Office of the Chairperson of the AU Commission, Addis Ababa, Ethiopia, 19 May 2006.

55   See Assembly/AU/9(VII) Add.2, p.4.

56   See Ex.CL/290(IX) Add.2

57   Interview with official, Legal Affairs Directorate, Ministry of Foreign Affairs, Addis Ababa, Ethiopia, 12 April 2006.

58   Transformation of the All Africa Ministerial Conference on Democratisation and Local Development to an Africa Union Structure, Executive Council, Ninth Ordinary Session 25–29 June 2006, Banjul, the Gambia, EX.CL/290(IX) Add.1.

59   Not one of the papers submitted in support of the agenda items proposed by Algeria, Congo or Mali in 2006 was ten pages long. The report by Mali on the 23rd Françafrique summit was actually the final statement of the meeting.

60   For example, the paper by Congo was just 2¼ pages long requesting a review of the mandate of the Commissioner in charge of Labour and Social Affairs (AssemblyAU/9(VII) Add.3.

61   The file submitted by Senegal on the Hissène Habré case was nearly 600 pages long, according to the ambassador of Senegal to the African Union.

62   Interview with official, Office of the Chairperson of the AU Commission, Addis Ababa, Ethiopia, 19 May 2006.

63   EX.CL/276(IX).

64   Interview with officials, Ministry of Foreign Affairs and Department of Africa and Asian Affairs, Gaborone, Botswana, 26 September 2006.

65   Interview with official, AU and Multilateral, Ministry of Foreign Affairs and Cooperation, Addis Ababa, Ethiopia, 12 October 2006.

66   The AU also recognises Africans in the diaspora as its '6th region'. The first Extraordinary Assembly of the AU, held in Addis Ababa, February 2003, agreed to add a new Article 3(q) to the Constitutive Act expanding the existing objectives of the Union, to: 'invite and encourage the full participation of the African Diaspora as an important part of our Continent, in the building of the African Union.'

67   Interview with officials, Ministry of Foreign Affairs and Department of Africa and Asian Affairs, Gaborone, Botswana, 26 September 2006.

68   Inputs at consultative meeting, Addis Ababa, 10–11 November 2006.

69   Interview, Faiza Mohamed, Equality Now, Equality Now, Nairobi, Kenya, 21 April 2006.

70   Interview, Khabele Matlosa, Electoral Institute of Southern Africa, 25 August 2006. See also by Matlosa a paper entitled 'Political Integration and Democracy in Africa: the Role of the African Union' delivered in September 2006.

71   As of 12 June 2006 the following member states were not in arrears: Algeria, Angola, Botswana, Ethiopia, Ghana, Mozambique, Rwanda, Saharawi Arab Democratic Republic, South Africa and Tanzania.

72   See Article 4 of Presidential Decree No. 2-404 of 26 November 2002 on the organisation of the central administration of the Ministry of Foreign Affairs of Algeria.

73   The terminology used in the constitutions of four civil law countries demonstrates a considerable difference in their approach. While the Constitution of Senegal solemnly affirms the Government's commitment to contributing to the achievement of African Unity and authorises the Government to 'sign agreements of association or community with any (other) African state including partial or total renunciation of sovereignty with a view to achieving African unity' (Article 89, Paragraph 2) and Mali devotes a whole part (Part 15) of its constitution to African Unity, the Algerian constitution only mentions the fact that Algeria belongs to Africa in its Preamble, whereas the constitution of Congo mentions in its preamble that the country intends to 'contribute to world peace as a member of the African Union'.

74   For historical reasons, particularly the role played by France, the former colonial power, in constitution-drafting – with the exception of Algeria, which drafted a socialist-inspired constitution at the time of its independence.

75   On these issues, see Ambassador Amadou Diop, former diplomatic adviser of Presidents Abdou Diouf and Abdoulaye Wade of Senegal, *Sénégal, repères et grandeur d'une diplomatie*, Éditions Sentinelles, 2006, pp.67–69.

76   Article 79, Paragraph 2, of the Algerian Constitution. Article 53 of the Malian Constitution is more explicit, since it provides that the Prime Minister 'leads and coordinates governmental action'. The Constitution of Congo is silent regarding the powers and duties of the Prime Minister. It merely provides that the President of the Republic may 'delegate certain of his powers' thereto and that the Prime Minister replaces the President of the Republic 'when the latter is absent from the national territory' (Article 24 of the Congolese Constitution).

77   Such was the case, for instance, of the Algerian Prime Minister who represented President Abdelaziz Bouteflika at part of the Banjul summit of July 2006.

78   Presidential Decree No. 02-403 of 26 November 2002 establishing the powers and duties of the Ministry of Foreign Affairs of Algeria; Decree 2003-137 of 31 July 2003 on the Organisation of the Ministry of Foreign Affairs, Cooperation and Francophonie of Congo, amended by Decree 2005-328 of 29 July 2005.

79   In Mozambique, which, though a Commonwealth country has a different legal tradition, there is a prime minister, but with not very substantial powers; the president is both the head of state and of government.

80   For example, the Algerian and Senegalese texts stipulate that actions by the Minister of Foreign Affairs shall be conducted 'under the authority of the President of the Republic' and that the Ministry of Foreign Affairs is the only ministerial department empowered to correspond with foreign countries or their representatives or with international organisations. Presidential Decree No. 02-403 of 26 November 2002 establishing the powers and duties of the Ministry of Foreign Affairs of Algeria and Decree No. 88-1697 of 16 December 1988 on the organisation of the Ministry of Foreign Affairs of Senegal. See also, Decree No. 2003-137 of 31 July 2003 on the Organisation of the Ministry of Foreign Affairs, Cooperation and Francophonie of Congo, amended by Decree No. 2005-328 of 29 July 2005; and Decree No. 00058/PRM of 21 February 2000 establishing the specific powers and duties of the members of the government of Mali.

81   Thus far, we have been unable to gain access to the decree organising this ministry. However, it should be noted that the minister has often been the official mediator of the Algerian government in charge of monitoring the peace process in the Democratic Republic of Congo and in the Great Lakes Region and the special envoy of the Algerian president to the president of Eritrea and the prime minister of Ethiopia.

82   Decree No. 00058 of 21 February 2000 establishing the powers and duties of the members of the government of Mali stipulates in Article 1 that the Minister of African Integration is mandated to promote and implement national policy relating to African integration and, is accordingly in charge of: implementing all initiatives and actions aimed at achieving African unity; and implementing the economic policy of economic integration in the framework of sub-regional or regional integration organisations.

83   For example, Article 3 of Presidential Decree No. 02-406 of 26 November 2002 establishing the powers and duties of the ambassadors of the Democratic and Popular Republic of Algeria requires the ambassador to 'assist national actors (enterprises, media

and non-governmental organisations) in their relations with foreign partners'.

84   Interview with officials, Africa and AU Directorate, Ministry of Foreign Affairs, Nairobi, Kenya, 18 April 2006; Africa Affairs and General Directorate, Ministry of Foreign Affairs, Addis Ababa, Ethiopia, 12 April 2006.

85   Interview with officials, Africa Affairs and General Directorate, Ministry of Foreign Affairs, Addis Ababa, Ethiopia, 12 April 2006.

86   Interview with officials, Africa and AU Directorate, Ministry of Foreign Affairs, Nairobi, Kenya, 18 April 2006; Africa Affairs, General Directorate, Ministry of Foreign Affairs, Addis Ababa, Ethiopia, 12 April 2006; and AU and Multi-lateral Department, Ministry of Foreign Affairs and Cooperation, Maputo, Mozambique, 12 October 2006.

87   The government departments responsible for education in South Africa and Kenya took the lead in formulating a government position in the respective countries. See interviews with officials, Africa Multi-lateral, Department of Foreign Affairs, Pretoria, South Africa, 7 June 2006; Africa and AU Directorate, Ministry of Foreign Affairs, 18 April 2006.

88   Interview with officials, Africa Multi-lateral, Department of Foreign Affairs, Pretoria, South Africa, 7 July 2006; and Office of the President, Gaborone, Botswana, 26 September 2006.

89   Interview with official, AU and Multi-lateral, Ministry of Foreign Affairs and Cooperation, Maputo, Mozambique, 12 October 2006.

90   Interview with official, East Africa Community Ministry, Nairobi, Kenya, 20 April 2006. The AU ordinarily consults the RECs for input ahead of the summit.

91   Inputs at consultative meeting, Addis Ababa, 10–11 November 2006.

92   Assembly/AU/Dec. 83(V), Sirte, Libya.

93   *Summary Report of the Working Group on the Draft Single Legal Instrument on the Merger of the African Court on Human and Peoples' Rights and the Court of Justice of the African Union*, UA/EXP/Fusion.cours/Rpt.(I), p.3.

94   Interview with official, Africa and AU Directorate, Ministry of Foreign Affairs, Nairobi, Kenya, 18 April 2006.

95   Interview with official, Africa and Middle East Division, Ministry of Foreign Affairs and Cooperation, Maputo, Mozambique, 12 October 2006.

96   Interview with technical adviser of the Ministry of Foreign Affairs of Mali, in Bamako, 24 August 2006.

97   See http://www.pmg.org.za. This website contains parliamentary committee meeting minutes, including those of the Foreign Affairs parliamentary committee, which has oversight of the Ministry of Foreign Affairs.

98   Interview with Member of Parliament and of the Pan-African Parliament, Nairobi, Kenya, 20 April 2006.

99   In Mali, it seems that the prime minister plays only a marginal role in determining the composition of the official delegation, which is a responsibility of the Office of the President of the Republic and the Ministry of Foreign Affairs. See above-mentioned interview with an adviser of the Minister of Foreign Affairs in Bamako.

100   Interview with official, Africa and AU Directorate, Ministry of Foreign Affairs, Nairobi, Kenya, 18 April 2006.

101   The *Association pour le Progrès et la Défense des Droits des Femmes* (APDF or Association for the Advancement and Defence of Women's Rights) whose representative was recently appointed ambassador to Germany, and the *Association des juristes maliennes* (AJM or Malian Association of Jurists).

102   Interview with the Senegalese Ambassador to the African Union, 6 October 2006.

103   Interview, Faiza Mohamed, Equality Now, Nairobi, Kenya, 21 April 2006.

104   A Regional Economic Community (REC) is defined as a regional grouping formed as a legal entity with the purpose to achieve economic, social and political integration. See Treaty Establishing the African Economic Community (1991).

105   The Treaty Establishing the African Economic Community, Article 88(1) reads: The community shall be established mainly through the coordination, harmonisation and progressive integration of the activities of the regional economic communities. Article 6 of the Treaty outlines six stages over 40 years from adoption of treaty to achieve full economic and political integration.

106   Economic Community of Central African States (11 members – Angola, Burundi, Democratic Republic of the Congo, Congo, Cameroon, Central African Republic, Chad, Equatorial Guinea, Gabon, Rwanda, Sâo Tomé and Principe); Economic Community of West African States (15 members – Benin, Burkina Faso, Cape Verde, Cote d'Ivoire, the Gambia, Ghana, Guinea Bissau, Guinea, Liberia, Mali, Nigeria, Niger, Senegal, Sierra Leone, Togo); Common Market for East and Southern African States (20 members – Burundi, the Comoros, the Democratic Republic of the Congo, Djibouti, Eritrea, Egypt, Ethiopia, Kenya, Libya, Malawi, Mauritius, Madagascar, Rwanda, the Seychelles, Swaziland, Somalia, Sudan, Uganda, Zambia, Zimbabwe); Inter-governmental Authority for Development (7 members – Djibouti, Eritrea, Ethiopia, Kenya, Somalia, Sudan, Uganda); Arab Maghreb Union (5 members – Algeria, Libya, Mauritania, Morocco, Tunisia); East African Community (three members – Kenya, Tanzania, Uganda); the Community of Sahelo-Saharan States (23 members – Benin, Burkina Faso, Central African Republic, Chad, Côte d'Ivoire, Djibouti, Egypt, Eritrea, The Gambia, Ghana, Guinea-Bissau, Liberia, Libya, Mali, Morocco, Niger, Nigeria, Senegal, Sierra Leone, Somalia, Sudan, Togo, Tunisia); Southern African Development Community (14 members – Angola, Botswana, Democratic Republic of the Congo, Lesotho, Malawi, Mauritius, Madagascar, Mozambique, Namibia, South Africa, Swaziland, Tanzania, Zambia, Zimbabwe). Other groupings that are not considered RECs are, for example, the Southern African Customs Union and the Manu River Union.

107   For example, Kenya is a member of the East African Community, the Common Market for East and Southern African States and the Inter-Governmental Authority for Development.

108   Chris Landsberg and Shaun Mackay, *Engaging the new Pan-Africanism: Strategies for Civil Society*, ActionAid International and Open Society Initiative for Southern Africa, 2004, p.12.

109   Constitutive Act of the African Union (2000), Article 3(l).

110   Draft Protocol on the Relationship between the Regional Economic Communities (REC) and the AU EX.CL/158(IX).

111   See Report on the Rationalisation of the Regional Economic Communities, Executive Council Ninth Ordinary Session, 25–29 June 2006, Banjul, the Gambia, EX.CL/278(IX) Rev.1. p.6.

112   Interview, Dr Kokerai, Legal Affairs Unit, SADC Secretariat, Gaborone, Botswana, 28 September 2006.

113   Interview, Dr Kokerai, Legal Affairs Unit, SADC Secretariat, Gaborone, Botswana, 28 September 2006.

114   See Mechanism for Coordination between the African Union and the Regional Economic Communities in the infrastructure sector, fifth meeting of the AU/RECs, Joint secretariat, 25–26 June 2006, Banjul, the Gambia, IE.D/01(V), Customs proposal on regional integration in Africa, 2nd Ordinary session of the AU-Sub-committee of Directors General of Customs, Harare, Zimbabwe 6–7 April 2006.

115   Declaration, First Conference of African Ministers of Integration, 30–31 March 2006, COMAI/Decl.(I).

116   Interview, Dr. Kokerai, Legal Affairs Unit, SADC Secretariat, Gaborone, Botswana, 28 September 2006.

117   Interview, M Mathiba-Madibela, Gender Unit, SADC Secretariat, Gaborone, Botswana, 28 September 2006.

118   Interview, Dr. A Mondlane, Policy and Strategic Planning Unit, SADC Secretariat, Banjul, the Gambia, 25 June 2006.

119   SADC summit meeting record, Maseru, Kingdom of Lesotho, 17–18 August 2006. The troika of the Organ is composed of Tanzania, Namibia and Angola.

120   According to the AU's five geographical regions, the Democratic Republic of the Congo (DRC) belongs to the Central African region. The DRC belongs to three RECs.

121   ECOWAS Bulletin, No. 1 October 2006.

122   Declaration and Treaty of the SADC.

123   Naefa Khan, 'Engaging SADC: A Discussion Paper on Civil Society Options', *Policy: Issues and Actors*, Vol. 19 No. 1., pp.4–5. Interview, Abie Ditlhake, SADC Council of NGOs, Gaborone, Botswana, 27 September 2006.

124   Proceedings Report, the 2nd SADC Civil Society Forum, theme, 'Democratic Governance and Regional Economic Integration,' hosted by SADC CNGO, 14–16 August, Maseru, Lesotho.

125   Interview, Alice Mogwe, Ditshwanelo, Gaborone, Botswana, 26 September 2006.

126   Naefa Khan, 'Engaging SADC: A Discussion Paper on Civil Society Options', *Policy: Issues and Actors*, Vol. 19. No. 1 (2006); *Major Achievements and Challenges: 1980–2005*, SADC, October 2005.

127   Interview, Dr Kokerai, Legal Affairs Unit, SADC Secretariat, Gaborone, Botswana, 28 September 2006.

128   Interview, Babolokile Tlae, Botswana Council of Non-governmental Organisations, Gaborone, Botswana, 27 September 2006.

129   *Interim Report on the Consultation: Strengthening Human Security Capacities of ECOWAS and West African Civil Society*, Abuja, Nigeria, May 30–June 1, 2003, ECOWAS Secretariat, International Alert and Centre for Democracy and Development. Available at http://www.wacsof.org/info/ECOWAS_interim_report.pdf.

130   Membership is drawn from organisations of diverse backgrounds and with experience in human security, education, trade, health democracy, good governance, human rights, gender equality, conflict transformation, trafficking in persons, transparency and anti-corruption.

131   See Article 8 of the Supplementary Protocol on Democracy and Good governance (2002), which calls on Member States to use the services of civil society organisations involved in electoral matters to educate and enlighten the public on the need for peaceful elections devoid of all acts of violence, Article 41(1)(a) of the Protocol relating to the Mechanism for Conflict Prevention, Management, resolution, Peace-keeping and Security (1999), which commits ECOWAS to cooperate with national and regional NGOs and religious organisations in the implementation of the provisions of the Protocol, Regulation C/REG/5/11/96 providing for the establishment of a Forum of Associations recognised by ECOWAS and Recommendation A/REC.1/5/11/96 calling for the mobilisation of various sections of the population.

132   In particular, DANIDA and DFID.

133   Article 3 of the Charter of the West African Civil Society Forum.

134   They are: ECOWAS and civil society organisations; food, agriculture and environment; gender issues; governance, democracy and human rights; Health, HIV-AIDS, and education; Media, telecommunications, and information technology; Peace and security; Policy research and database; regional integration, economic development, trade and investment; youth. See Article 8(2) and (3) of the Charter of the West African Civil Society Forum.

135   Article 6(3) of the Charter of the West African Civil Society Forum.

136   The Forum may also meet in extraordinary session under conditions specified in Article 6(3)(b) of the Charter of the West African Civil Society Forum.

137   Article 8 of the Charter of the West African Civil Society Forum.

138   Article 8(2) and (3) of the Charter of the West African Civil Society Forum.

139   Final Communiqué of the 28th summit of the ECOWAS; Paragraphs 117 & 118 of the final report of the 53rd ordinary session of the Council of Ministers of ECOWAS.

140   The first Forum took place in Accra (11–12 December 2003), the second in Accra (10–13 January 2005) and the third in Niamey (4–6 January 2006).

141   Recommendations made by WACSOF available at http://www.wacsof.org.

142   Including to Benin, Burkina Faso, Gambia, Ghana, Guinea Bissau, Liberia and Togo. A pre-election evaluation mission was also sent to Cote d'Ivoire.

143   Communiqué of the Constitutive Assembly of the West African Civil Society Forum, p.2.

144   Recommendations of the West African Civil Society Forum adopted in Niamey (January 2006) to the ECOWAS Council of Ministers, p.4.

145   In a press statement of 17 January 2006, the *Fédération Internationale des Ligues de droits de l'homme* (FIDH) noted that 'a recommendation of the ECOWAS NGO Forum adopted in January 2006 demanded the extradition of of President Habré in order to respect the right to a fair process and the right to justice for his victims'. This was not quite correct in respect of the content of the WACSOF recommendations.

146   These weaknesses are reflected in the recommendation of the WACSOF meeting held in Niamey in 2006 inviting member states to 'respect their commitments to end slavery, trafficking in and exploitation of children ... [and] to encourage education and information of citizens on these inhuman practices and to end them', which could have been adopted by any meeting of human rights organisations. WACSOF should have rather been more precise on the routes of trafficking in persons, the role of the institutions of certain member states, and demanded specific rather than vague actions by the heads of state and government and the ECOWAS organs.

147   Inputs at consultative meeting, Addis Ababa, 10–11 November 2006.

148   See generally, 'Brainstorming session on Building an African Union for the Twenty First Century, 25–28 October 2003, Addis Ababa, Ethiopia: Involving civil society in the building of the African Union – Introductory note', pp.3–4.

149   CSSDCA Solemn Declaration, Lomé, Togo, July 2000, AHG/Decl.4(XXXVI); Decision on the Conference on Security, Stability, Development and Cooperation in Africa, AHG/Dec.175(XXXVIII), approving the Memorandum of Understanding on Security, Stability, Development and Cooperation in Africa.

150   Brainstorming session on 'Building an African Union for the Twenty First Century', p.4.

151   See, *Salvador Declaration: Conference of Intellectuals from Africa and the Diaspora*, July 12–14, 2006, Salvador, Bahia, Brazil.

152   Report of the Commission for the period January – June 2006, Executive Council, Ninth Ordinary Session, 25–29 June 2006, Banjul, the Gambia, EX.CL/271(IX), p.4. Also Opening address to the 3rd African Union-Civil Society (AU-CSO) Forum, Banjul, the Gambia, 20–21 June 2006, delivered by Dr Jinmi Adisa, Africa Citizens Directorate (CIDO), Bureau of the Chairperson, African Union Commission. Rules of Procedure of the Peace and Security Council of the AU, Rule 15(2) reads: '(b) the Council may decide to hold open meetings and may invite to participate, without a right to vote, in the discussion under consideration and regional mechanism, an international organisation or civil society organisation, which is involved/interested in a conflict or situation related to the discussion under consideration by the Council.'

153   Opening address to the 3rd African Union-Civil Society Forum delivered by Dr Jinmi Adisa.

154   Quoted in Irungu Houghton, *Reflections on African Union, NEPAD and African CSO engagement with an eye on Continental Citizenship, Public Accountability and Governance*, December 2005.

155   Inputs at consultative meeting, Addis Ababa, 10–11 November 2006.

156   Opening address to the 3rd African Union-Civil Society Forum, Banjul, the Gambia, 20–21 June 2006, delivered by Dr Jinmi Adisa, head, African Citizens' Directorate (CIDO), Bureau of the Chairperson, African Union Commission.

157   Telephone interview with official, Africa Renaissance Organisation for Southern Africa and Secretary General for the South Africa chapter of ECOSOCC, 26 July 2006; interview, Helder Malauene, Foundation for Community Development and member of the Interim Standing Committee, Maputo, 10 October 2006.

158   Resolution and Recommendations of the Third AU-CSO Forum held in Banjul, the Gambia to the Seventh Ordinary Session of the Assembly of State and Government, 21 June 2006.

159   Inputs at consultative meeting, Addis Ababa, 10–11 November 2006.

160   Report on the Elaboration of a Framework Document on Post Conflict Reconstruction and Development (PCRD), Executive Council Ninth Ordinary session 25–26 June 2006, Banjul, the Gambia, EX.CL/274(IX).

161   Solidarity for African Women's Rights, 'Update on the Campaign on Ratification, Domestication and Popularisation of the Protocol on the Rights of Women in Africa,' Equality Now, April to June 2006.

162   Information supplied by Faiza Mohamed, Equality Now, November 2006.

163   Interview, Binta Diop, *Femmes Afrique Solidarité*, November 2006.

164   See, 'Implementation of the *Solemn Declaration On Gender Equality In Africa*: First Report by all AU Member States, for consideration at the January 2007 summit to be held in Addis Ababa, Ethiopia', at http://www.africa-union.org/root/au/Conferences/Past/2006/October/WG/doc.htm.

165   The single-chamber Pan-African Parliament may provide a further opportunity for civil society to influence AU policy-making, especially when it ceases being a purely advisory body and assumes its legislative duties in 2009. However, its operations were not researched for the purposes of this report.

166   Constitutive Act of the AU (2001), Article 5(1)(h).

167   Constitutive Act of the AU (2001), Article 22 reads: '(1) The Economic, Social and Cultural Council shall be an advisory organ composed of different social and professional groups of Member States of the Union.' The definition of the ECOSOCC constituency is still not entirely clear: for example, the status of faith-based organisations within ECOSOCC is being clarified.

168   Chris Landsberg and Shaun Mackay, *Engaging the New Pan Africanism: Strategies for Civil Society*, Action Aid International and Open Society Initiative for Southern Africa, 2004, p.30.

169   Report on the Regional Consultative Forum on ECOSOCC, Pretoria, South Africa, 18–19 November 2003.

170   Decision on the Economic, Social and Cultural Council (ECOSOCC), Assembly/AU/Dec.48(III).

171   Statutes of the Economic, Social and Cultural Council of the African Union, Article 2.

172   Statutes of the Economic, Social and Cultural Council of the African Union, Article 6(6). The criteria include other less controversial requirements such as registration in an African country, provision of annual audited statements, etc.

173   Statutes of the Economic, Social and Cultural Council of the African Union, Article 9(2)(d).

174   Interview, James Shikwati, director of the Inter-Region Economic Network and the national coordinator for the Kenya chapter of ECOSOCC, Nairobi, Kenya, 19 April 2006.

175   Draft Report of the Official Launching of the Interim General Assembly of the Economic, Social and Cultural Council (ECOSOCC), Interim General Assembly of the Economic, Social and Cultural Council, 26–30 March 2005, Addis Ababa, Ethiopia, INT/ASSEMBLY/ECOSOCC/DRAFT/RPT(I).

176   The interim bureau consists of the interim president and four interim deputy presidents: Fatima Karadja (north Africa); Charles Mutasa (southern Africa); Ayodele Aderinwale (west Africa); and Maurice Tadadjeu (central Africa).

177   Interim Standing Committee members are: Jean Collins Musonda Kalusambo, *Solidarité pour la Jeunesse* Asbl-ONGD, Democratic Republic of Congo; Julienne Mavoungou Makaya, CARESCO, Republic of Congo; Yvette N Rekangalt, *Union des ONG du Gabon*; Zeinab Kamel Ali, National Committee for Human Rights, Djibouti; El Hussein Abdel Galil Mohammed, Freedom Equality Peace Society, Sudan; Patrick Kayemba, DENIVA, Uganda; Amany Asfour, Egyptian Business Women's Association, Egypt; Saida Agrebi, Association of Tunisian Mothers, Tunisia; Ahmed Abdel Fattah, Sahrawi Youths Union; Moses Tito Kachima, Southern Africa Trade Union Coordination Council, Botswana; Joyce Nondwe Kanyago, National Women's Coalition, South Africa; Helder Francisco Malauene, Foundation for Community Development, Mozambique; Mama Koite Doumbia, *Syndicat National de l'Education et de la Culture*, Mali; Landing Badji, *Ligue Africaine des Droits de l'Homme et des Peuples*, Senegal; Omar Gassama, National Youth Council, The Gambia.

178   Draft report of the official launching of the Interim General Assembly of the Economic, Social and Cultural Council (ECOSOCC), Interim General Assembly of the Economic, Social and Cultural Council, 26–30 March 2005, Addis Ababa, Ethiopia, INT/ASSEMBLY/ECOSOCC/DRAFT/RPT(I).

179   Interview, Helder Malauene, Foundation for Community Development and Interim Standing Committee member, Maputo, Mozambique, 11 October 2006.

180   Draft Decision on Transitional Arrangements for the Launching of the Economic, Social and Cultural Council (ECOSOCC) of the African Union. The decision reads: 'In order to ensure the speedy launching of ECOSOCC, the Commission shall convene a General Civil Society Conference which shall serve as the Interim General Assembly of ECOSOCC pending the election and setting up of the General Assembly.'

181   Opening address to the 3rd African Union-Civil Society (AU-CSO) Forum, Banjul, the Gambia, 20–21 June 2006, delivered by Dr. Jinmi Adisa, Head, African Citizens' Directorate CIDO, Bureau of the Chairperson, African Union Commission.

182   Inputs at consultative meeting, Addis Ababa, 10–11 November 2006.

183   Interview, Moses Kachima, Southern African Trade Union Coordination Council, Gaborone, Botswana, 27 September 2006, Interview, Omar Gassama, National Youth Council, Banjul, the Gambia, 24 June 2006. Both respondents serve on the Interim Standing Committee.

184   Interview, Helder Malauene, Foundation for Community Development and Interim Standing Committee member, Maputo, Mozambique, 11 October 2006.

185   Interview, Moses Kachima, Southern African Trade Union Coordination Council and member of the Interim Standing Committee of ECOSOCC, Gaborone, Botswana, 27 September 2006; interview, Abie Ditlhake, Southern African Development Community Council of Non-governmental Organisations, Gaborone, Botswana, 27 September 2006.

186   Inputs at consultative meeting, Addis Ababa, 10–11 November 2006.

187   Report of the Commission for the period January–June 2006, Executive Council, Ninth Ordinary Session, 25–29 June 2006, Banjul, the Gambia, EX.CL/271(IX), p.4; see also ECOSOCC Statutes, Article 5.

188   Invitation from AFRODAD and Idasa to participants, 14 November 2006; Report of the Commission for the period January–June 2006, Executive Council Ninth Ordinary Session, 25–29 June 2006, Banjul, the Gambia, EX.CL/271(IX) p. 4.

189   Interview, James Shikwati, director, Inter-Region Economic Network and national coordinator for Kenya chapter of ECOSOCC, 19 April, Nairobi, Kenya, 2006.

190   Interviews, Steve Ouma, Kenya Human Rights Commission, Nairobi, Kenya, 20 April 2006; Faiza Mohamed, Equality Now, Nairobi, Kenya, 21 April 2006; Roselynn Musa, FEMNET, Nairobi, Kenya, 20 April 2006.

191   Telephone interview, Zanele Mkhwanazi, South African Non-Governmental Organisation Coalition (SANGOCO), 30 August 2006.

192   Telephone interview, Tshepo Mashiane, African Renaissance Organisation for Southern Africa and Secretary General for the South Africa chapter of ECOSOCC, 26 July 2006.

193   Ibid.

194   Telephone interview, Zanele Mkhwanazi, South African Non-Governmental Organisation Coalition (SANGOCO), 30 August 2006; interview, Gillian Ayong, Action Support Centre, Johannesburg, South Africa, 25 August 2006.

195   Interview with official, Africa Multi-lateral, Department of Foreign Affairs, Pretoria, South Africa, 7 June 2006.

196   Ibid., 192 above.

197   Interviews, Chris Landsberg, Centre for Policy Studies, Johannesburg, South Africa, 10 July 2006; Gillian Ayong, Action Support Centre, South Africa, 25 August 2006. Khabele Matlosa, Electoral Institute of Southern Africa, Johannesburg, South Africa, 25 August 2006; Email communication, Corlett Letlojane, Human Rights Institute of South Africa, 6 October 2006.

198   Interview, Alice Mabote, Liga dos Direitos Humanos, Maputo, Mozambique, 11 October 2006.

199   Interview, Helder Malauene, Foundation for Community Development and Interim Standing Committee member, Maputo, Mozambique, 11 October 2006.

200   Ibid.

201   Interview, Omar Gassama, National Youth Council and member of the Interim Standing Committee of ECOSOCC, Banjul, the Gambia, 24 July 2006.

202   Interview, Ousmane Yabo, the Association of NGOs, Johannesburg, South Africa, 25 June 2006.

203   Interviews, Alice Mogwe, Ditshwanelo, Gaborone, Botswana, 26 September 2006; Babolokile Tlale, Botswana Council of

Non-governmental Organisations, 28 September 2006.

204   Interview with officials, Africa Affairs, General Directorate, Ministry of Foreign Affairs, Addis Ababa, Ethiopia, 12 April 2006.

205   Interview, Helen Seifu, Ethiopia Women Lawyers Association, Addis Ababa, Ethiopia, 12 April 2006; Tamre Teka, PANOS Ethiopia, Addis Ababa, Ethiopia, 16 May 2006.

206   Interview, Steve Ouma, Kenya Human Rights Commission, Nairobi, Kenya, 20 April 2006.

207   Interview, Khabele Matlosa, Electoral Institute of Southern Africa, Johannesburg, South Africa, 25 August 2006.

208   In Geneva, the International Service for Human Rights plays such a role in relation to the UN structures there. There have been discussions among some funders, including the Open Society Institute and Trust Africa, about the possibility of supporting a similar institution in Addis Ababa.

209   http://www.africa-union.org/.

210   http://www.nepad.org/.

211   See http://www1.worldbank.org/operations/disclosure/ for the World Bank's policy.

212   See, 'International tribunal makes landmark ruling on access to information', Open Society Justice Initiative, 12 October 2006.

213   Interviews, Faiza Mohamed, Equality Now, Nairobi, Kenya, 21 April 2006; Roselynn Musa, FEMNET, Nairobi, Kenya, 20 April 2006.

214   Interview with official, AU and Africa Directorate, Nairobi, Kenya, 18 April 2006.

215   Interview, Gillian Ayong, Action Support Centre, Johannesburg, South Africa, 25 August 2006.

216   Inputs at consultative meeting, Addis Ababa, 10–11 November 2006.

217   Interview, Gillian Ayong, Action Support Centre, Johannesburg, South Africa, 25 August 2006. Interview, Roselynn Musa, FEMNET, Nairobi, Kenya, 20 April 2006.

218   Inputs at consultative meeting, Addis Ababa, 10–11 November 2006.

219   Inputs at consultative meeting, Addis Ababa, 10–11 November 2006.

220   Criteria for granting observer status and for a system of accreditation within the AU, EX/CL/195(VII). The document also sets out rules for non-African states and organisations to be accredited with the AU.

221   The meeting was organised by a coalition led by CREDO (the Centre for Research Education and Development of Rights in Africa) and hosted by FEMNET. The aim of the meeting was 'to develop an effective demand and partnership platform for African CSOs in the African Union and other inter-governmental processes affecting the continent'. Concept Paper for an Independent African Civil Society Consultation, 2005; interview, Rotimi Sankore, CREDO, 29 November 2006. See also, Wangui Kanina, 'African Union help sought to try former Chad ruler', Reuters, 16 January 2006.

222   *Drums of Change*, Quarterly Newsletter of the Peace and Development Platform, Vol. 1, Issue 1, June 2004, p.5. Also, interview, Gillian Ayong, Action Support Centre (the Peace and Development Platform is a programme of Action Support Centre), Nairobi, Kenya, 25 August 2006.

223   Interview, Ousmane Yabo, the Association for NGOs, Banjul, the Gambia, 25 June 2006.

224   Interview, Helder Malauene, Foundation for Community Development and ECOSOCC Interim Standing Committee member, Maputo, Mozambique, 11 October 2006; Email communication from Viriato Teotónio e. Tamele, Economic Justice Coalition, Maputo, January 2007.

225   Interviews, Gillian Ayong, Action Support Centre, Johannesburg, South Africa, 25 August 2006; Ousmane Yabo, the Association for NGOs, Banjul, the Gambia, 25 June 2006; inputs at consultative meeting, Addis Ababa, 10–11 November 2006.

226   Inputs at consultative meeting, Addis Ababa, 10–11 November 2006.

227   Edmund Blair, 'Rights delegates released in Sudan', Reuters, 21 January 2006. The coalition Solidarity for African Women's Rights, however, did successfully hold a symposium in Khartoum.

228   Free Expression and Journalist Organisations Prevented from Holding Forum on Freedom of Expression', Press Statement, Media Foundation for West Africa, 23 June, 2006.

229   Declaration on Unconstitutional Changes of Governance in Africa, Doc. EX.CL/258(IX), 2000.

230   OAU/AU Declaration on the Principles Governing Democratic Elections in Africa, AHG/Decl.1(XXXVIII), 2002.

231   Africa Conference on Governance, Democracy and Elections adopts Programme of Action, Press Statement, 10 April 2003.

232   Draft Charter on Democracy, Elections and Governance: Explanatory Note, available at http://www.africa-union.org/root/au/conferences/past/2006/april/pa/apr7/meeting.htm.

233   Inputs at consultative meeting, Addis Ababa, 10–11 November 2006.

234   See http://www.hrw.org/justice/habre/ for background on the case.

235   Official statement by the Ministry of Foreign Affairs of Senegal, 27 November 2005.

236   Note of introduction for the item on the agenda of the 6th Session of the Assembly of the African Union, proposed by Senegal and entitled 'The Hissène Habré case and the African Union' (Assembly/AU/8(VI) Add.9.

237   Interview, 30 December 2005.

238   Decision on the Hissène Habré case, Assembly/AU/Dec.103(VI)

239   *Rapport du Comité d'éminents juristes africains sur l'affaire Hissène Habré.* Undated, unreferenced document by the African Union. The committee's members were: Judge Gibril Camara, Senegal; President Delphine Emmanuel née Adouki, Congo Brazzaville; Professor Ayodele Ajomo, Nigeria; Adv. Robert Dossou, Benin; Judge Joseph Warioba, Tanzania; Adv. Anil Kumarsingh Gayan, Mauritius; and Professor Henrietta Mensa-Bonsu, Ghana.

240   Decision on the Hissène Habré case and the African Union, Assembly/AU/Dec.127(VII).

241   Constitutive Act, Article 4(h). The Committee further stipulated that 'its task was to help establish a mechanism to fight against impunity, specifically in the African framework'. See *Rapport du Comité d'éminents juristes africains sur l'affaire Hissène Habré.*

Undated, unreferenced document of the African Union, p.2.

242   See Article 6, Paragraph 4 of the Constitutive Act of the African Union. In Article 5 of the Protocol on Amendments to the Constitutive Act of the African Union (not yet in force), it is specified that the election takes place during an ordinary session of the Union, that the choice is made on a rotating basis and that the mandate is renewable.

243   See Article 15, Paragraph 2 of the Rules of Procedure of the Assembly of the African Union. However, where the January summit is exceptionally convened outside Addis Ababa (as in January 2006), the hosting of that session is not linked to the presidency of the Union. Decision on the Framework for the Organisation of Future Summits, Assembly/AU/Dec.63(IV).

244   Assembly/AU/Dec.54(III).

245   Assembly/AU/Dec.53(III).

246   Paragraph 6 of the Decision in Assembly/AU/Dec.63(IV).

247   At the Abuja summit, the Heads of State and Government decided that henceforth the January session, during which the acting chairperson of the Assembly would be elected, would be held at the headquarters of the Union, in Addis Ababa, unless the Assembly decided otherwise, following a recommendation by the Executive Council; Assembly/AU/Dec.63(IV).

248   'East Africa backs Bashir as AU head – Sudanese official', Reuters, 19 January 2006.

249   Interview with official, Legal Affairs Directorate, Ministry of Foreign Affairs, Addis Ababa, Ethiopia, 12 April 2006.

250   Interview with officials, Office of the President, Gaborone, Botswana, 26 September 2006; and Ministry of Foreign Affairs and Department of Africa and Asian Affairs, 26 September 2006.

251   Interview with official, Office of the President, Gaborone, Botswana, 26 September 2006. The committee included, in addition to Botswana, which acted as chair, Burkina Faso, Djibouti, Egypt, Gabon, Tanzania and Zimbabwe.

252   Assembly/AU/Recommendation(VI); see also 'Mogae returns from Khartoum' Republic of Botswana, *Tautona Times*, 25 January 2006.

253   'Decision on AU presidency must take into account the vital role of the AU as mediator and guarantor of protection for the people of Darfur', Darfur Consortium press release, 21 January 2006.

254   Assembly/AU/Dec.6(II).

255   Resolutions on the human rights situation in Ethiopia, on the human rights situation in the Darfur region of Sudan, on the human rights situation in Uganda and on the human rights situation in Zimbabwe adopted during the 38th ordinary session of the African Commission on Human Rights.

256   Decision on the Activity Report of the African Commission on Human and Peoples' Rights, Assembly/AU/Dec.101(VI). The Assembly also decided that, in future, the African Commission should 'enlist the responses of all States parties to its Resolutions and Decisions before submitting them to the Executive Council and/or the Assembly for consideration' and that states should 'within three months of the notification by the African Commission on Human and Peoples' Rights, communicate their responses to Resolutions and Decisions to be submitted to the Executive Council and/or the Assembly'.

257   See 20th Activity Report of the African Commission on Human and Peoples' Rights, EX.CL/279(XI), pp.38–110.

258   The Ugandan delegate referred to a 'loss of confidence in the African Commission', whereas the delegate from Ethiopia stressed 'the arrogance of the African Commission'.

259   Communication No. 245/2002, *Zimbabwe Human Rights NGO Forum v Zimbabwe*. This is one of 13 complaints against Zimbabwe before the African Commission as of 30 May 2006.

260   See the 20th Activity Report of the African Commission on Human and Peoples' Rights, EX.CL/279(XI), pp.140–141 (on the response of the State as to the admissibility of the complaint) and pP.152–159 (on the response of the State on the merits of the case).

261   Article 59(1),(2) and (3), African Charter on Human and Peoples' Rights. The African Commission on Human Rights took care to have this viewpoint endorsed by the Commission of the African Union during the Brainstorming Session organised by the latter on 9–10 May 2006 at Banjul. (See 20th Activity Report of the African Commission on Human and Peoples' Rights, EX.CL/279(XI), pp.24–37.

262   See Decision on the Activity Report of the African Commission on Human and Peoples' Rights in EX.CL/Dec.310(IX)

263   Doc.EX.CL/252(IX).

264   Assembly/AU/Dec.118(VII).

265   Assembly/AU/Dec.64(IV).

266   'AU launches people's court', UN IRIN, 3 July 2006.

267   Decision on the Report of the 9th Extraordinary session of the executive council on the proposals for the Union Government, DOC.Assembly/AU/10 (VIII), Assembly/AU/Dec.156 (VIII).

268   *Study on an African Union Government: Towards a United States of Africa*, 2006.

269   Decision on the Union Government, Doc. Assembly/AU/2(VII).

270   Draft Report of the Continental Civil Society Conference on the Proposed African Union Government: Accelerating Africa's Integration and Development in the 21st Century: Prospects and Challenges of Union Government, Accra, Ghana, June 22–23 2007.

271   SADC Extra-ordinary summit meeting record, 23 October 2006, Midrand, South Africa.

272   See Decision on the report of the Chairperson on the Strengthening of the Commission, EX.CL/DEC.341 (X) which recommends the convening of an extraordinary session of the Executive Council to consult further on the contents of the AU Commission chairperson's report on strengthening the AU Commission.

273   Accra Declaration, Assembly of the Union at its 9th Ordinary session in Accra, Ghana, 1–3 July 2007. At the 10th Extra-ordinary session of the Executive Council of the African Union in South Africa, 10 May, foreign ministers had also agreed to conduct an audit of the AU Commission and the organs of the AU.

274   The members of the panel are: Prof. Adebayo Adedeji (Chair); Dr Fatima Zohra Karadjaa (Algeria); Dr Frene Ginwala (South Africa); Amb. Vijay Makhan (Mauritius); Mr Akere Tabeng Muna (Cameroon); Dr Makha Dado Sarr (Senegal); Mr Fahrat Bengdara (Libya); Ms Julienne Ondziel-Gnelenga (Congo); Amb. Netumbo Nandi-Ndaitwah (Namibia); Amb. Nana Affa Apenteng (Ghana); Hakim Ben Hammouda (UN Economic Commission on Africa); Prof. Abdala Bujra (Kenya); and Prof. Adebayo Olukoshi (CODESRIA).

275   Terms of reference of the Audit Review Panel, EX.CL/328(X) Annex IV.

276   Decision on the Ministerial Committee on Elections of the Members of the Commission, EX.CL/291(IX);

277   Report of the 10ᵗʰ Extraordinary Session of the Executive Council of the African Union, Zimbali, South Africa, 10 May 2007, Ext/EX.CL/Draft/Rpt (X).

278   Assembly/AU/Dec.168(IX)

279   The first three functions assigned to the Commission are (a) represent the Union and defend its interests under the guidance of and as mandated by the Assembly and the Executive Council; (b) initiate proposals for consideration by other organs; (c) implement the decisions taken by other organs. Article 3, Statutes of the Commission of the African Union, ASS/AU/2(I)d, 2002.

280   Report of AU/CSO Pre-Summit Forum, Accra, Ghana, 19–21 June 2007. The Executive Council extended the mandate of the Interim ECOSOCC to 31 December to allow for elections, (Decision on the Report of the Interim Economic, Social and Cultural Council (ECOSOCC), EX.CL/Dec.338 (X).

281   According to Article 12 of the ECOSOCC statutes, the Credentials Committee comprises the following: one CSO representative from each of the five regions in Africa, one CSO representative from the Diaspora; one nominated representative for special interest groups such as vulnerable groups; and two representatives of the Commission.

282   Draft Report of the Credentials Committee Meeting of the ECOSOCC, M-Plaza Hotel, Accra, Ghana, 17–20 June 2007.

283   According to a note circulated by the ECOSOCC Secretariat on 7 August 2007, the countries from which no nominations were received were: Angola, Benin, Botswana, Burundi, Cape Verde, Central African Republic, Chad, the Comoros, Congo, Djibouti, Eritrea, Equatorial Guinea, the Gambia, Guinea, Guinea Bissau, Lesotho, Liberia, Libya, Mali, Mauritania, Mozambique, Namibia, Saharawi Republic, Sao Tomé and Principé, Senegal, the Seychelles, Sierra Leone, Somalia, Swaziland, Rwanda, Tanzania, Togo and Zimbabwe.

284   See Conclusions and Decisions of the Interim Standing Committee, 3 September 2007,www.africa-union.org/root/au/AUC/Department/BCP/CIDO/meeting/October/ecosocc/ECOSOCC_election.

285   Ibid.

286   The organisations were: Pan African Women's Organisation (Angola); African Women's Development Communication Network (FEMNET, Kenya); Pan African Lawyers Union (PALU, Cameroon); Femmes Afrique Solidarité (FAS, Sénégal); Organisation of African Trade Union Unity (OATUU, Ghana); Pan-African Employers' Confederation (Kenya); Network of African Peace Builders (NAPS, Zambia); Africa Internally Displaced Persons Voice-Africa (IDP Voice, Zambia).

287   Charles Mutasa, 'Revisiting ECOSOCC', Pambazuka, 31 October 2007, available at http://www.pambazuka.org/aumonitor/comments/peoples_audit_revisiting_ecosocc/.

288   This clause was introduced at the insistence of Permanent Representatives during the approval of the ECOSOCC Statutes. If this criterion were applied to the AU Commission, a number of directorates and departments, including CIDO, would not be eligible to participate in AU affairs.